Non-verbal Reasoning
Rapid Tests 3

Rebecca Brant

Schofield & Sims

Introduction

This book gives you practice in answering non-verbal reasoning questions quickly.

The questions are like the questions on the 11+ and other school selection tests. You must find the correct answers.

School selection tests are usually timed, so you need to get used to working quickly. Each test has a target time for you to work towards. You should time how long you spend on each test, or you can ask an adult to time you.

All the questions in this book are multiple choice. For each question you are given a choice of answers. Choose the answer you think is correct and draw a circle round the letter beneath it.

What you need

- A pencil
- An eraser
- A clock, watch or stopwatch
- A sheet of rough paper
- An adult to help you work out how long you take and to mark the test for you

What to do

- Turn to **Section 1 Test 1** on page 4. Look at the grey box at the top of the page labelled **Target time**. This tells you how long the test should take.
- When you are ready to start, write down the time or start the stopwatch. Or the adult helping you will tell you to begin.
- Find this black arrow ⬇ near the top of the first page. Start each test here.
- Find this square ▪. The instructions for the first set of questions are beside it. Read them carefully.
- Look below the instructions. Read the **Example**. Work out why the answer given is correct.
- Using similar methods, answer each question.
- Try to answer every question. If you do get stuck on a question, leave it and go on to the next one. Work quickly and try your best.
- When you have finished the first page, go straight on to the next page without waiting. Here you may find a different question type. Again, read the instructions and the example. Then answer the questions.
- When you reach the end, stop. Write down the time or stop the stopwatch. Or tell the adult that you have finished.
- With the adult, work out how long you took to do the test. Fill in the **Time taken** box at the end of the test.
- The adult will mark your test and fill in the **Score** and **Target met?** boxes.
- Turn to the **Progress chart** on page 40. Write your score in the box and colour in the graph to show how many questions you got right.
- Did you get some questions wrong? You should always have another go at them before you look at the answers. Then ask the adult to check your work and help you if you are still not sure.
- Later, you will do some more of these tests. You will soon learn to work through them more quickly. The adult who is helping you will tell you what to do next.

Published by **Schofield & Sims Ltd**,
7 Mariner Court, Wakefield, West Yorkshire WF4 3FL, UK
Telephone 01484 607080
www.schofieldandsims.co.uk
First published in 2014
This edition copyright © Schofield & Sims Ltd, 2018
Fifth impression 2021

Author: **Rebecca Brant**. Rebecca Brant has asserted her moral right under the Copyright, Designs and Patents Act, 1988, to be identified as the author of this work.

British Library Cataloguing in Publication Data. A catalogue record for this book is available from the British Library.

All rights reserved. No part of this publication may be reproduced, stored in a retrieval system, or transmitted in any form or by any means, electronic, mechanical, photocopying, recording or otherwise, without either the prior permission of the publisher or a licence permitting restricted copying in the United Kingdom issued by the Copyright Licensing Agency Ltd.

Commissioned by **Carolyn Richardson Publishing Services**
Design by **Oxford Designers & Illustrators**
Front cover design by **Ledgard Jepson Ltd**
Printed in the UK by **Page Bros (Norwich) Ltd**
ISBN 978 07217 1465 3

Contents

Section 1	**Test 1**	Similarities, Odd one out	4
	Test 2	Analogies, Series	6
	Test 3	Hidden pictures, Reflected pictures	8
	Test 4	Matrices, Combined pictures	10
	Test 5	Nets of cubes	12
	Test 6	Codes	14
Section 2	**Test 1**	Nets of cubes, Codes	16
	Test 2	Combined pictures, Similarities	18
	Test 3	Odd one out, Analogies	20
	Test 4	Series, Hidden pictures	22
	Test 5	Matrices, Reflected pictures	24
	Test 6	Nets of cubes, Codes	26
Section 3	**Test 1**	Similarities, Odd one out	28
	Test 2	Analogies, Series	30
	Test 3	Hidden pictures, Reflected pictures	32
	Test 4	Matrices, Combined pictures	34
	Test 5	Nets of cubes, Codes	36
	Test 6	Hidden pictures, Series	38
Progress chart			40

A **pull-out answers section** (pages A1 to A8) appears in the centre of this book, between pages 20 and 21. It also gives simple guidance on how best to use this book. Remove this section before the child begins working through the tests.

Section 1 Test 1

Target time: 6 minutes

Which picture on the right belongs to the group on the left? Circle the letter.

Example

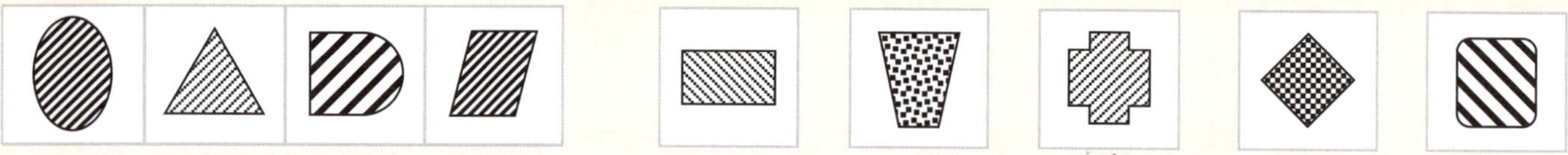

a   b   (c)   d   e

1.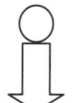

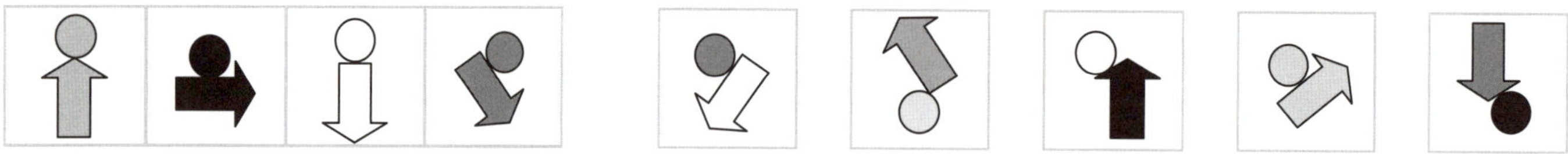

a   b   c   d   e

2.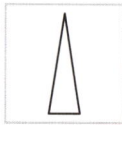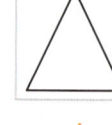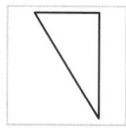

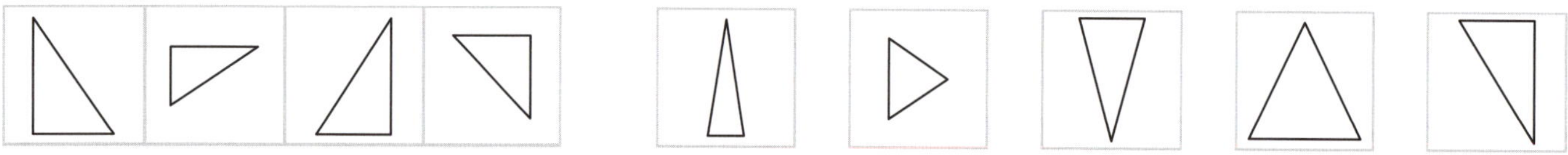

a   b   c   d   e

3.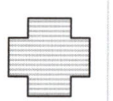

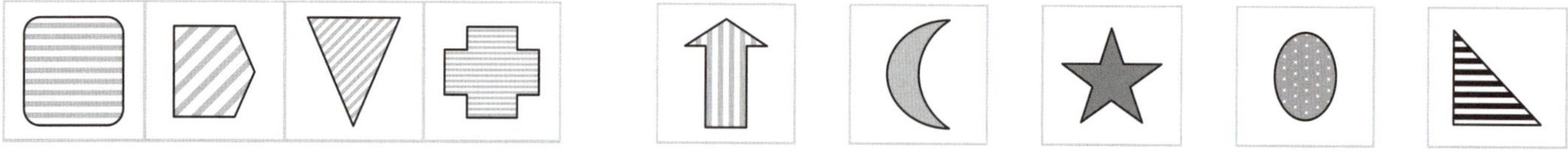

a   b   c   d   e

4.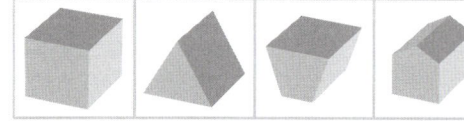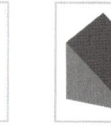

a   b   c   d   e

5.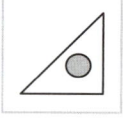

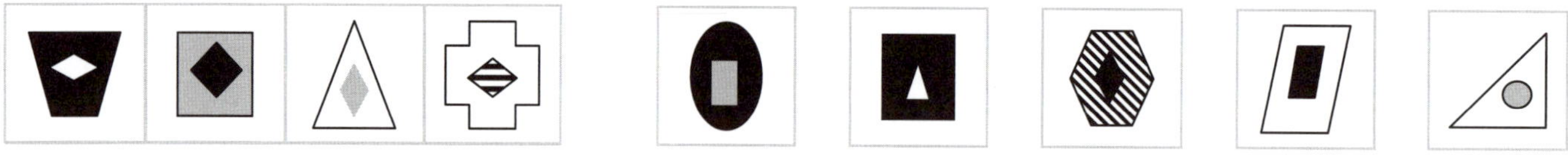

a   b   c   d   e

6.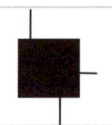

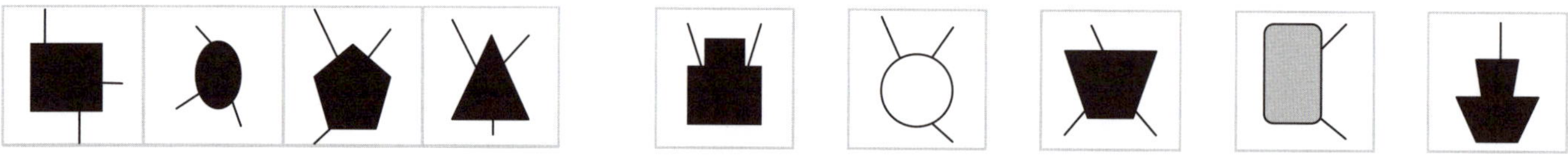

a   b   c   d   e

Now go on to the next page ➡

Section 1 Test 1 continued

Which picture is the odd one out? Circle the letter.

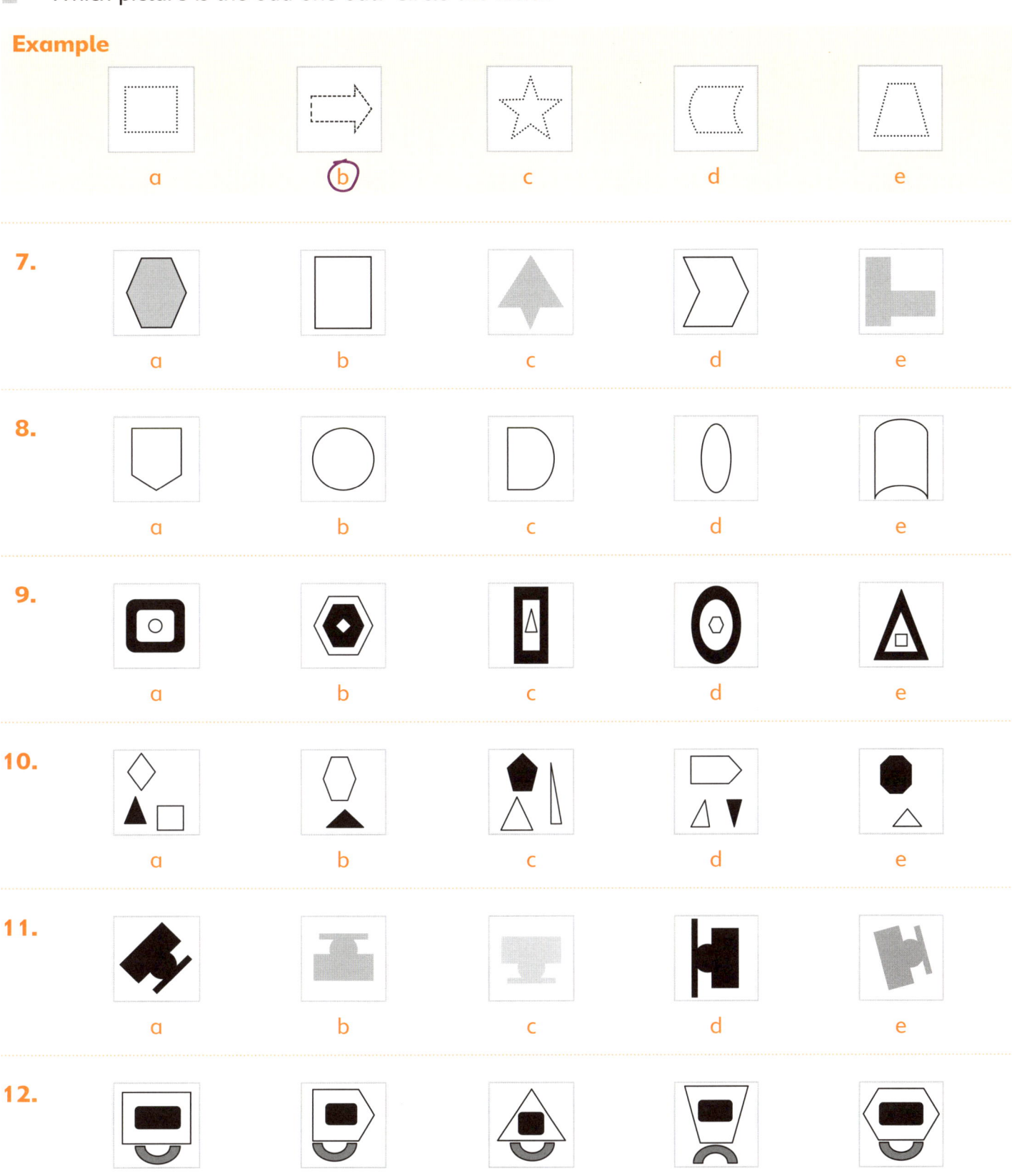

End of test

Section 1 Test 2

Target time: **6 minutes**

There is a pair of pictures on the left. Which one of the five pictures on the right goes with the single picture on the left to make a pair in the same way? Circle the letter.

Example

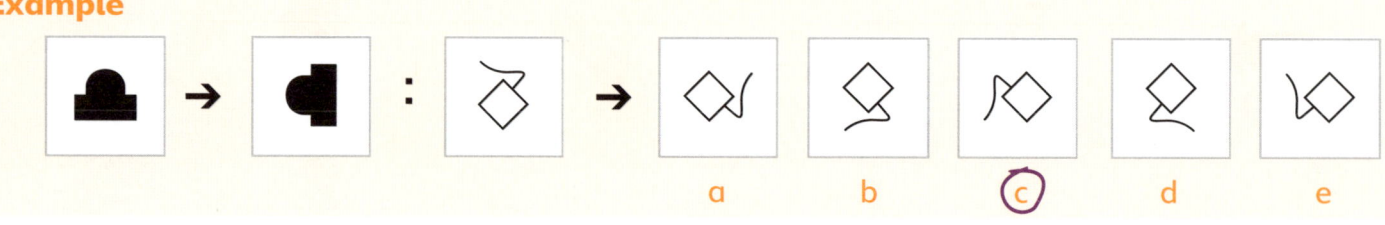

1.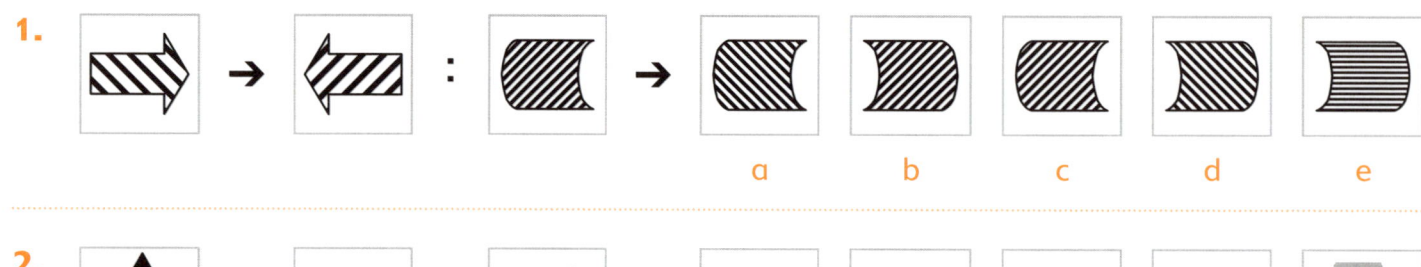

2.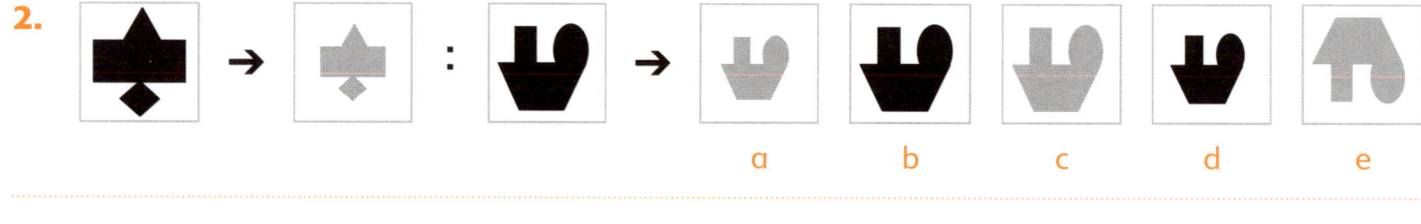

3.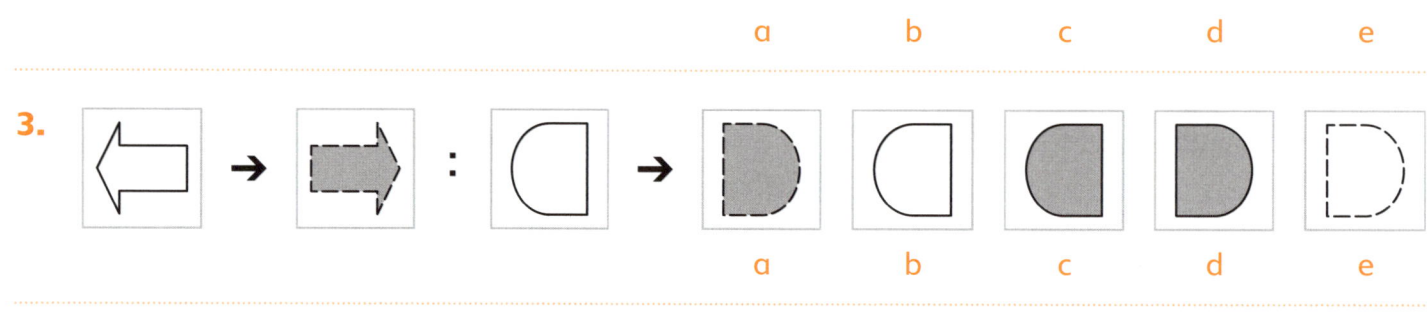

4.

5.

6.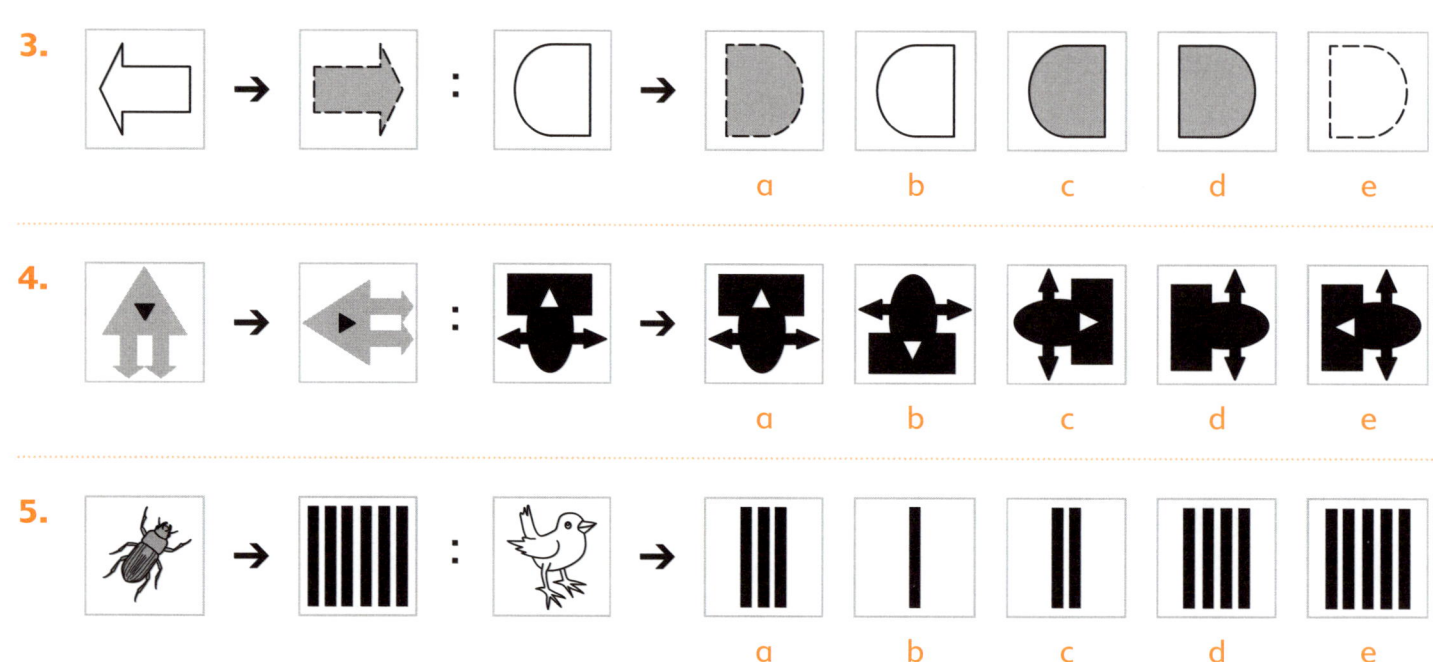

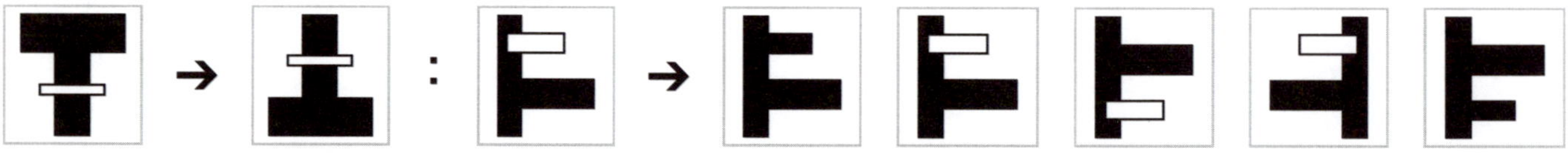

Now go on to the next page ➡

6   Schofield & Sims

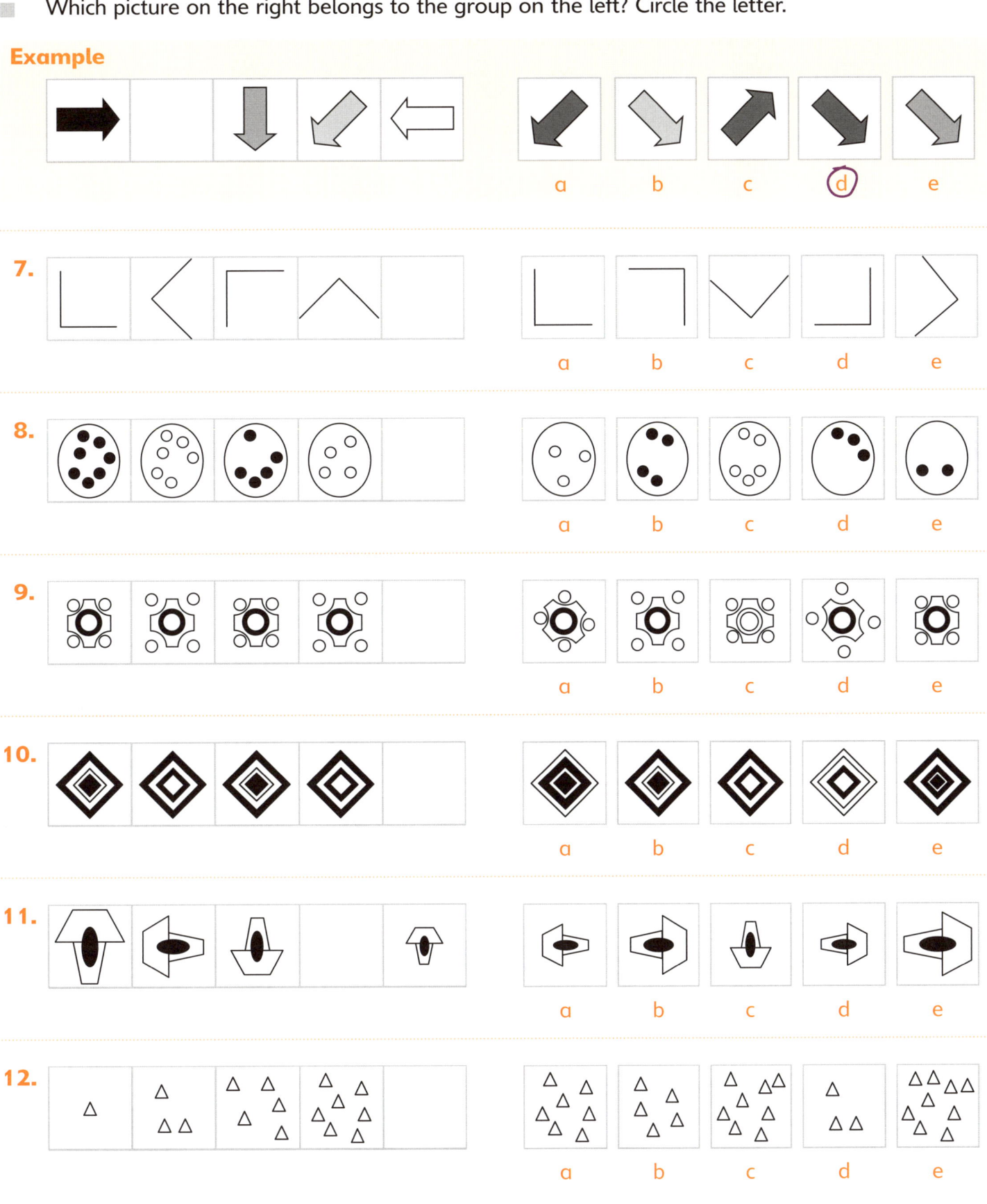

Section 1 Test 3

Target time: **6 minutes**

 In which picture on the right is the picture on the left hidden? Circle the letter.

Example

     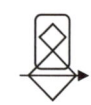      
                   a   b   c   d   (e)

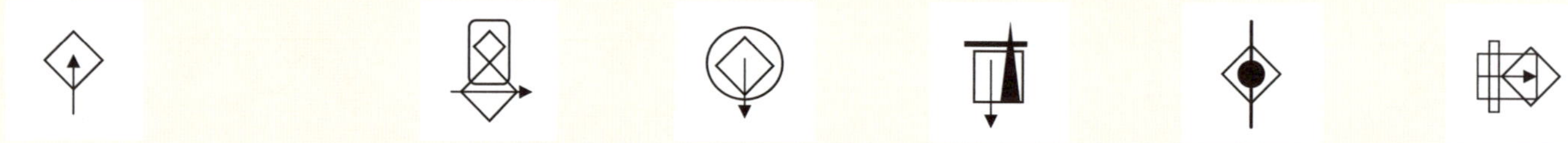

1.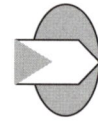
    a   b   c   d   e

2.
    a   b   c   d   e

3.
    a   b   c   d   e

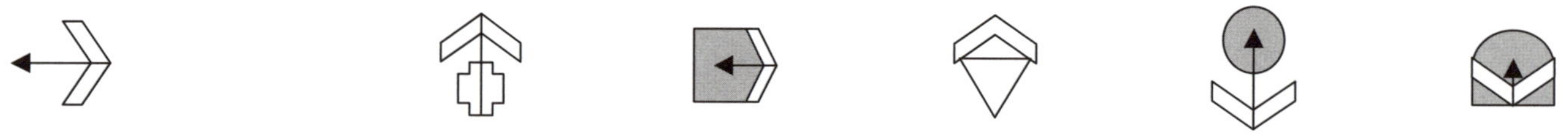

4.
    a   b   c   d   e

5.
    a   b   c   d   e

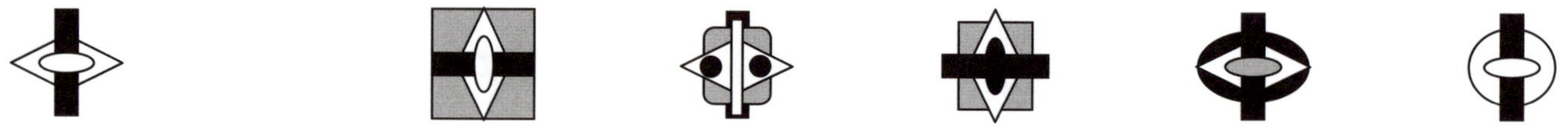

6.
    a   b   c   d   e

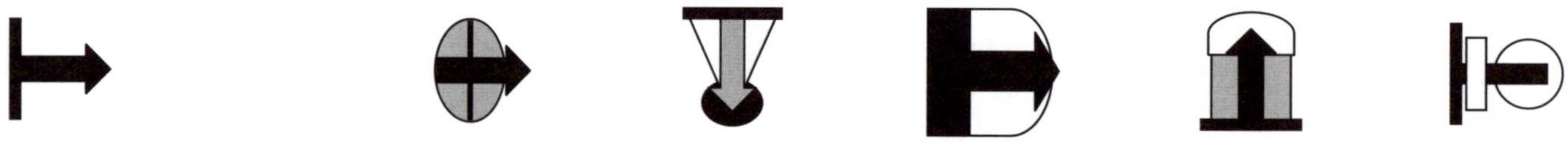

Now go on to the next page ➡

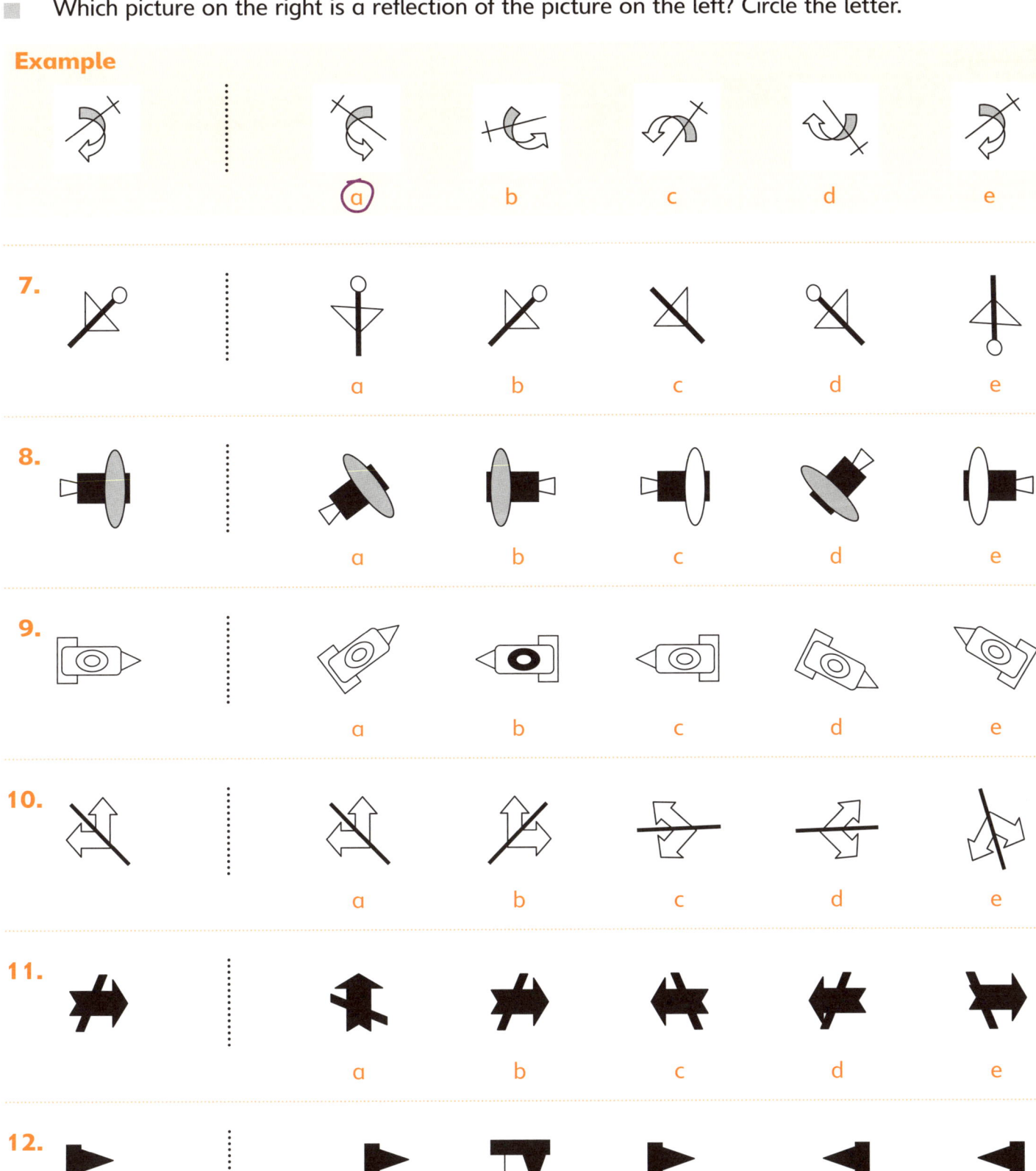

Section 1 Test 4

Target time: 6 minutes

 Which picture on the right best fits into the space in the grid on the left? Circle the letter.

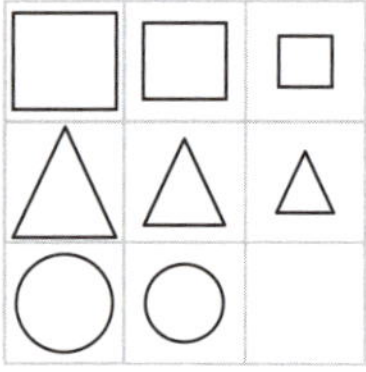

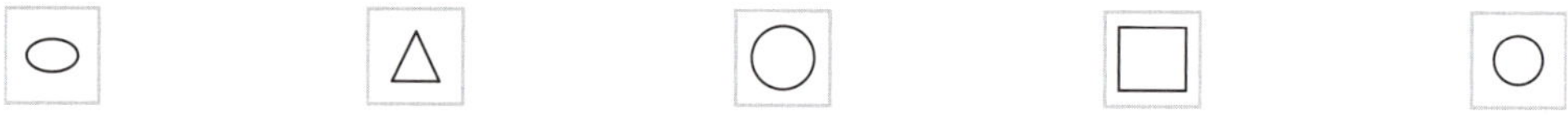

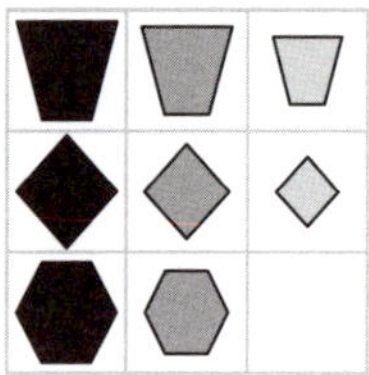

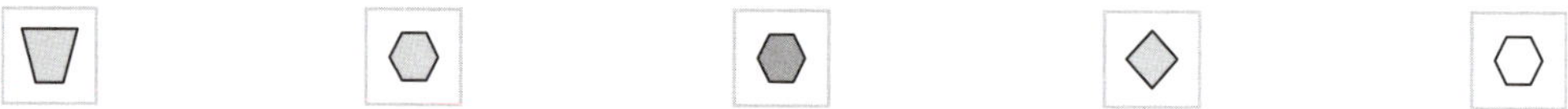

Example

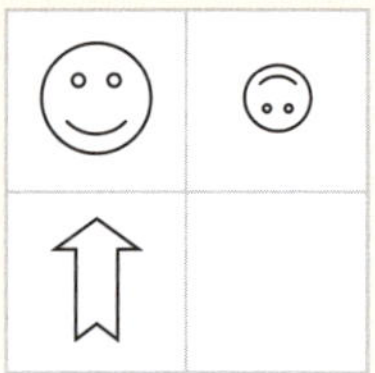

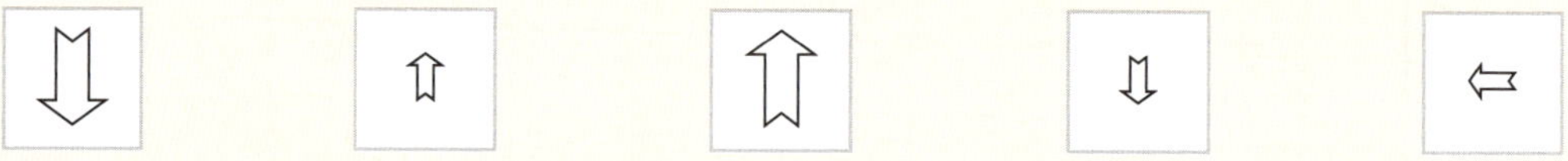

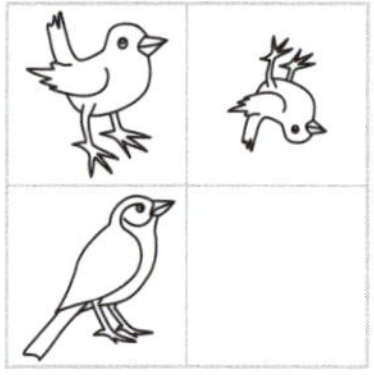

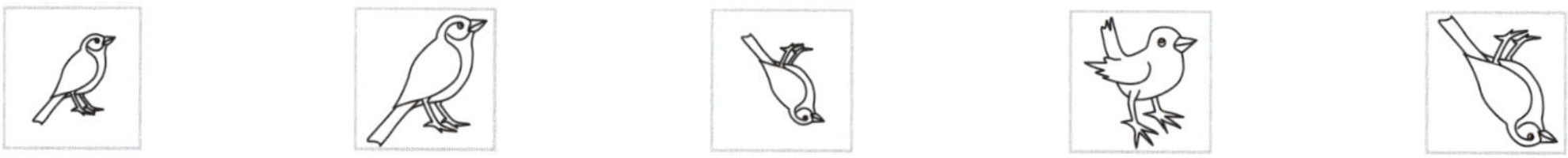

The answer is **d**.

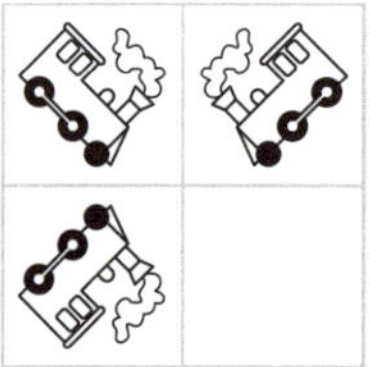

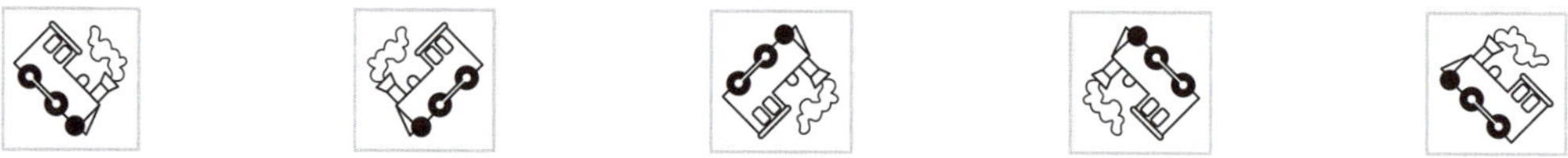

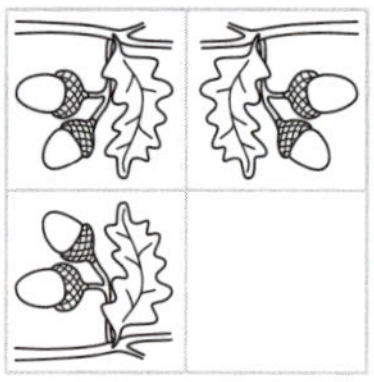

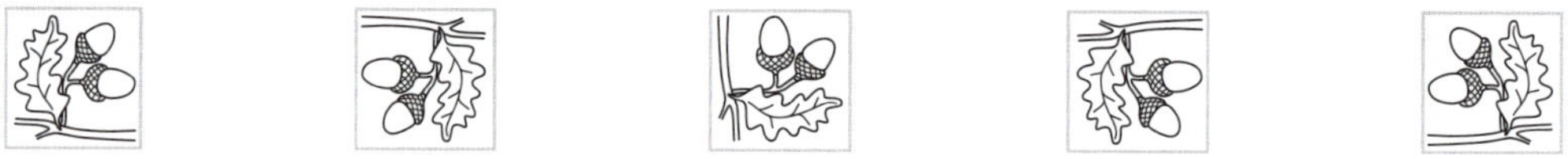

1.
2.
3.
4.
5.
6.

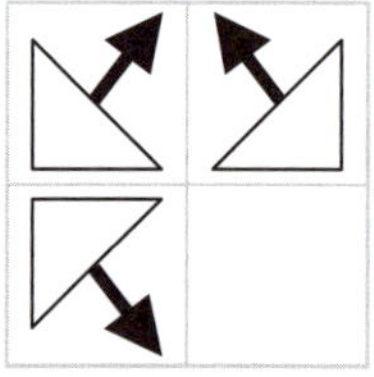

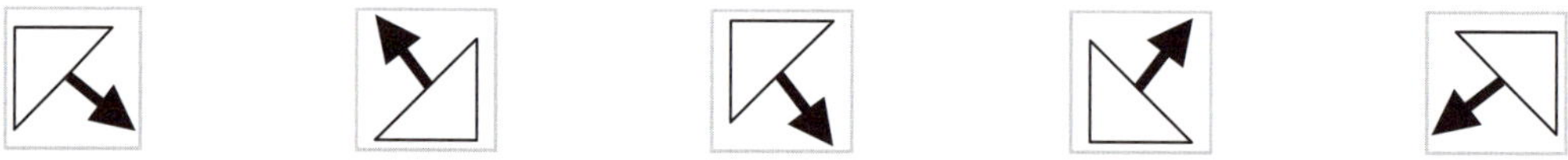

Now go on to the next page ➡

Section **1** Test **4**
continued

Which picture on the right can be made by combining the two shapes on the left? Circle the letter.

Example

 + 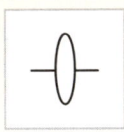 =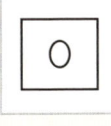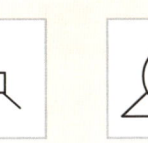
a b (c) d e

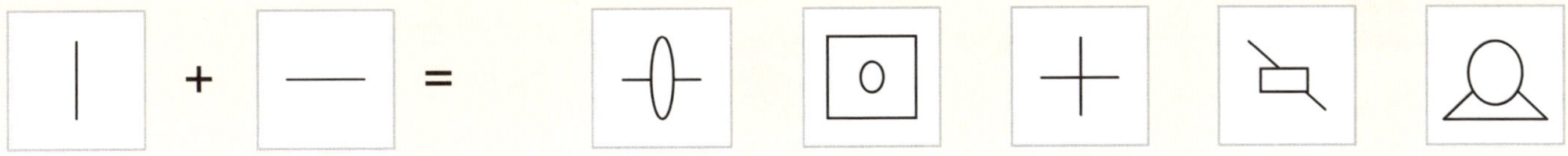

7. + =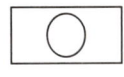
a b c d e

8. 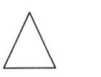 +  =
a b c d e

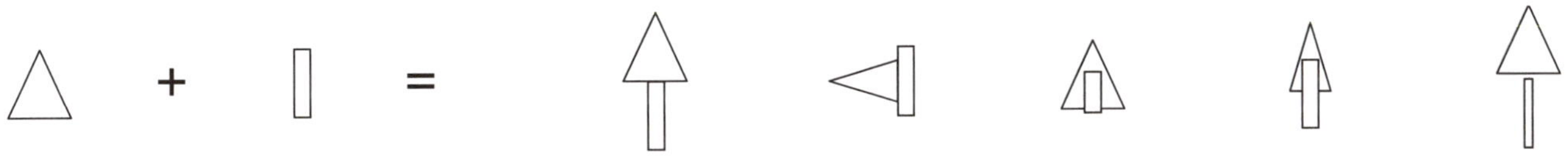

9. + 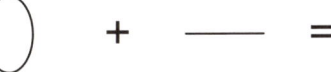 =
a b c d e

10. + 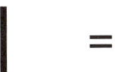 =
a b c d e

11. + =
a b c d e

12. +  =
a b c d e

End of test

Score: Time taken: Target met?

Non-verbal Reasoning Rapid Tests 3

Section 1 Test 5

Target time: **6 minutes**

Which cube can be made from the net? Circle the letter.

Example

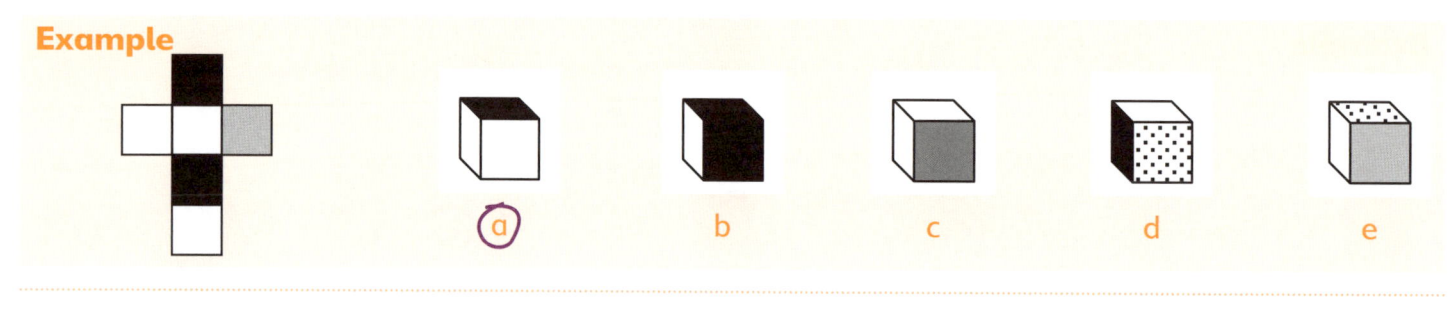

a (circled)   b   c   d   e

1. a b c d e

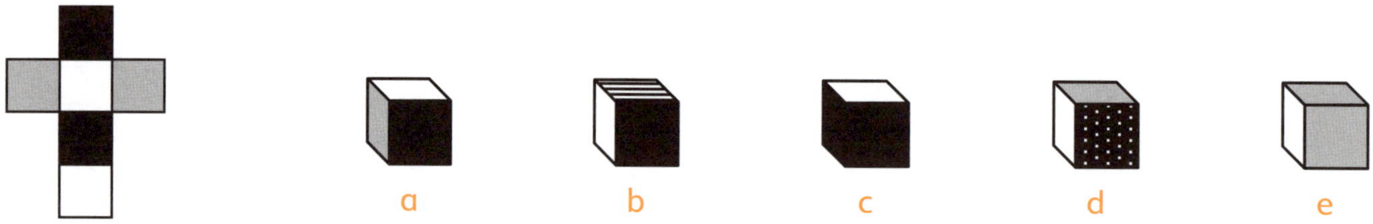

2. a b c d e

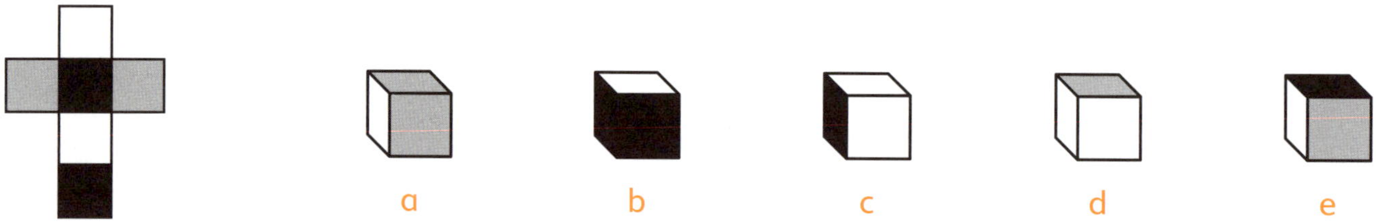

3. a b c d e

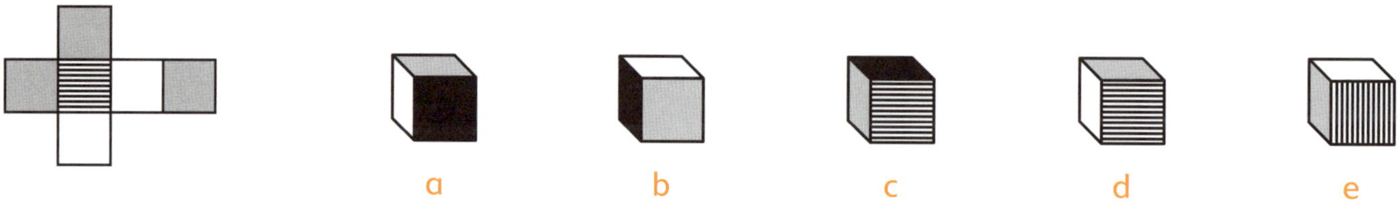

4. a b c d e

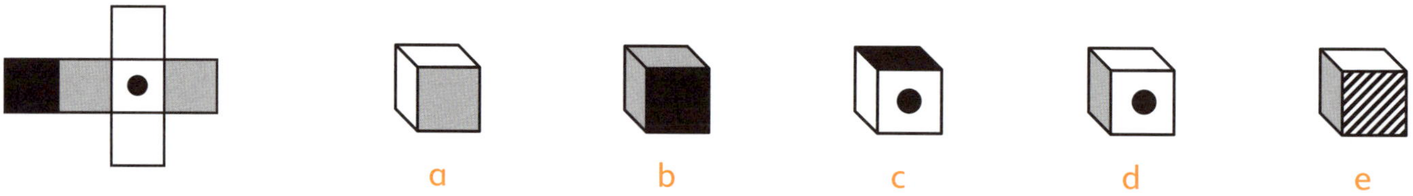

5. a b c d e

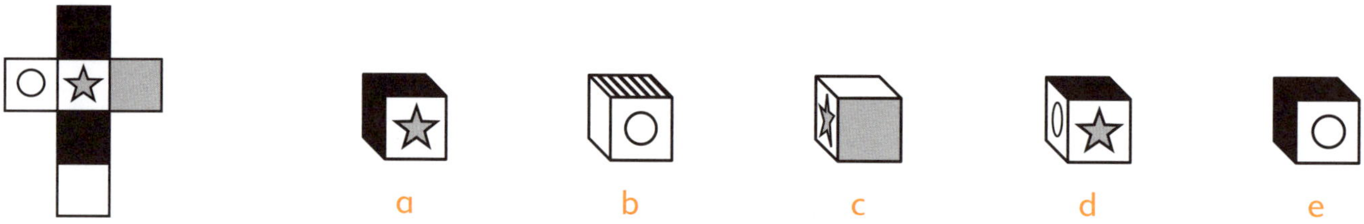

6. a b c d e

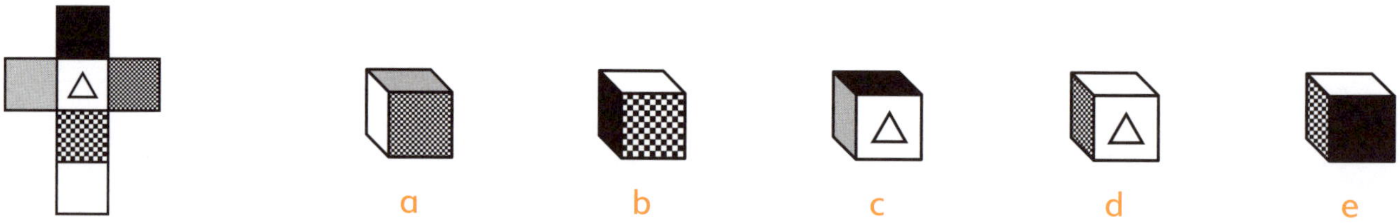

Now go on to the next page ➡

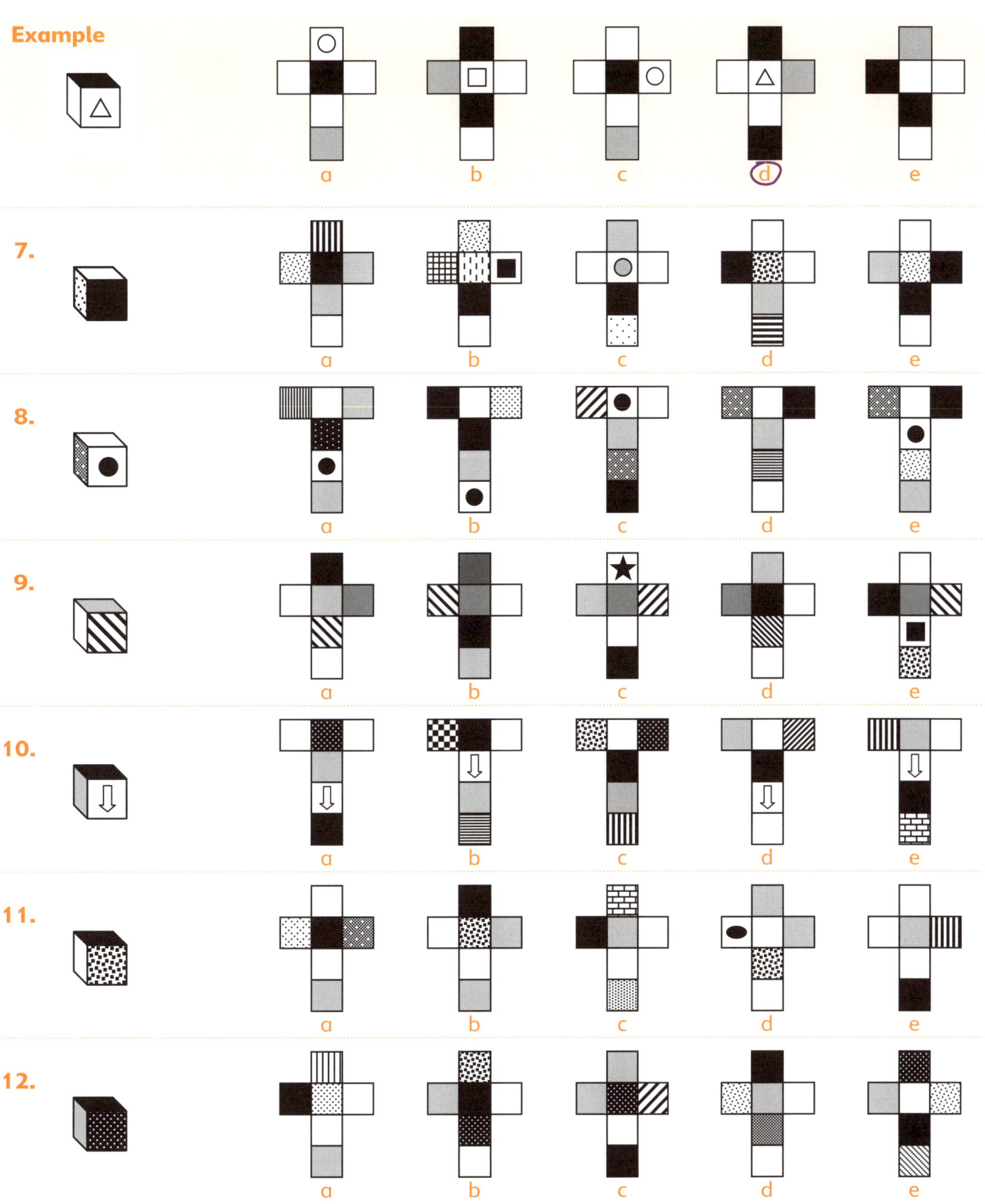

Section 1 Test 6

Target time: 6 minutes

What is the code of the final picture? Circle the letter.

Example

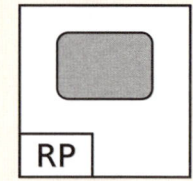 RP   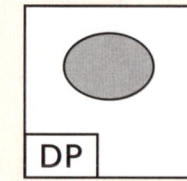 DP   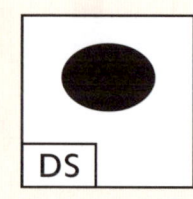 DS
DR | RS | RP | DS | PS
a   b   c   d   e

1.  HE   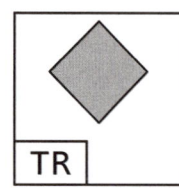 TR   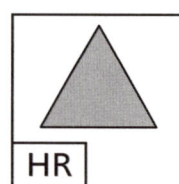 HR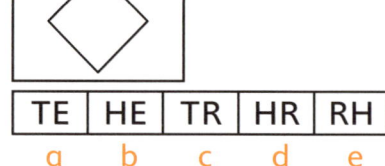
TE | HE | TR | HR | RH
a   b   c   d   e

2. 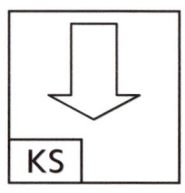 KS   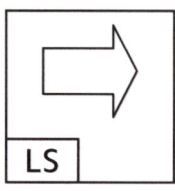 LS    KV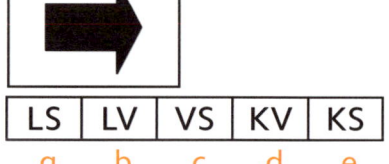
LS | LV | VS | KV | KS
a   b   c   d   e

3. 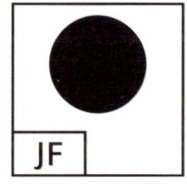 JF   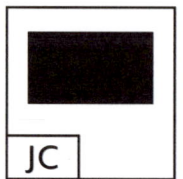 JC   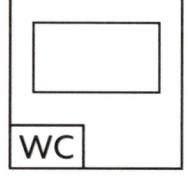 WC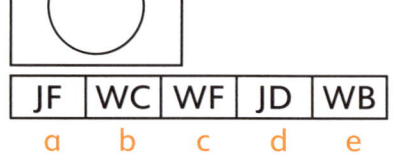
JF | WC | WF | JD | WB
a   b   c   d   e

4. 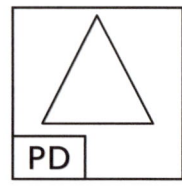 PD   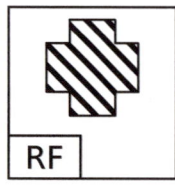 RF    PF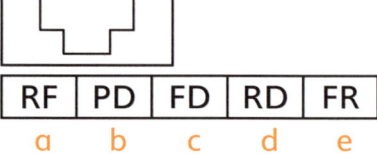
RF | PD | FD | RD | FR
a   b   c   d   e

5.  TY    NZ    TZ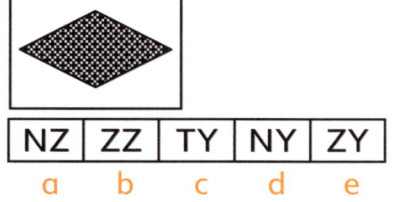
NZ | ZZ | TY | NY | ZY
a   b   c   d   e

Now go on to the next page ➡

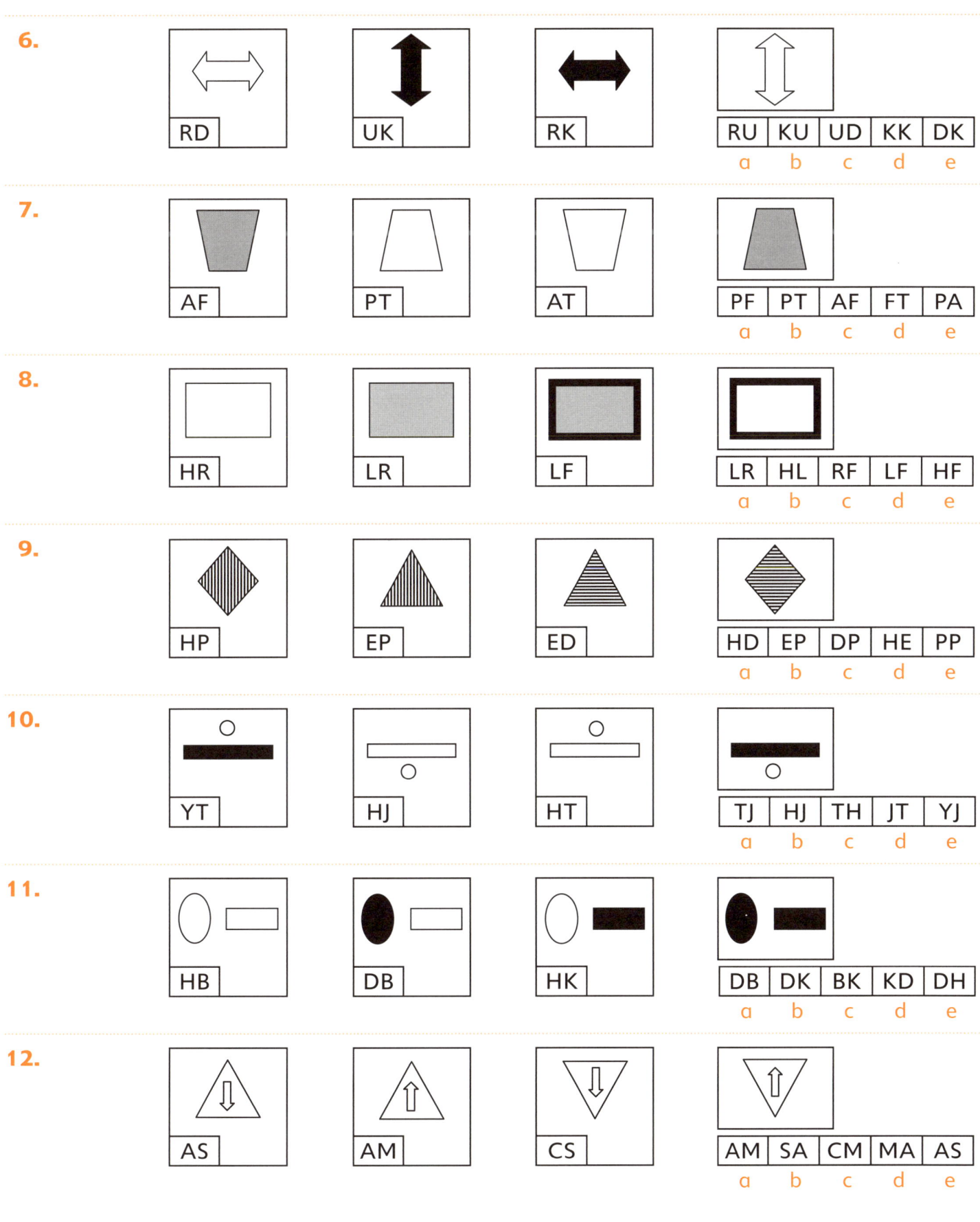

Section 2 Test 1

Target time: **6 minutes**

 Which cube can be made from the net? Circle the letter.

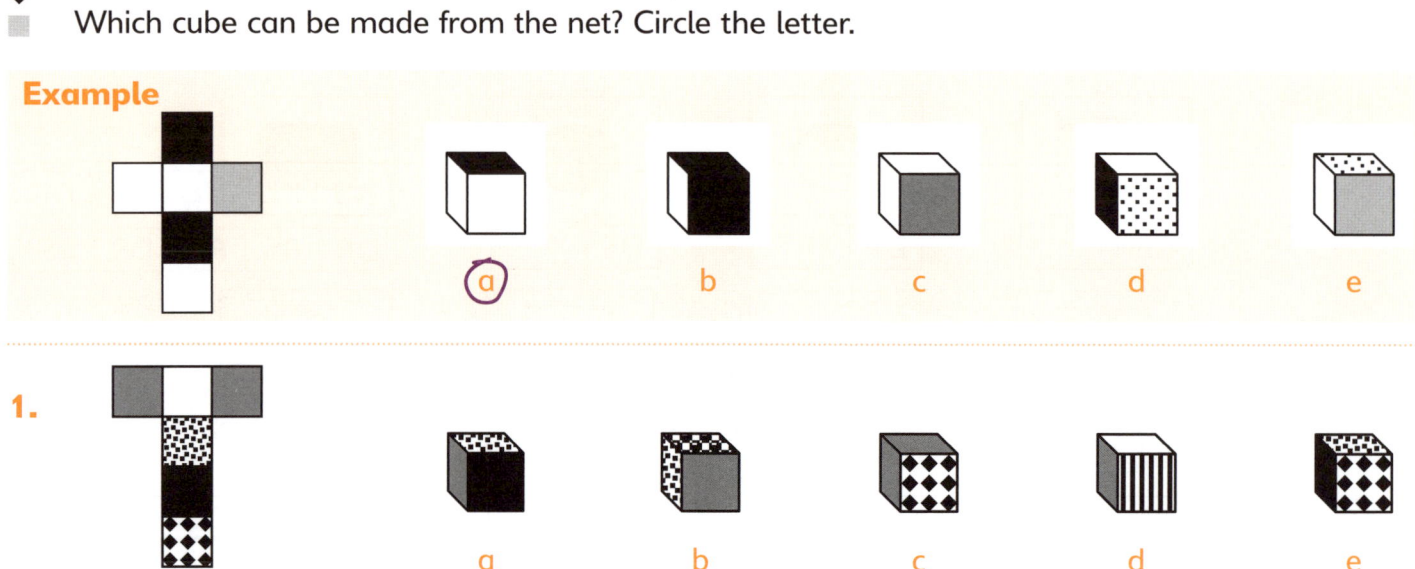

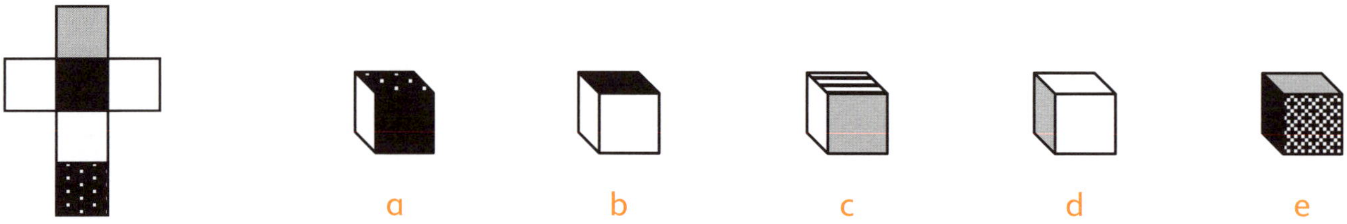

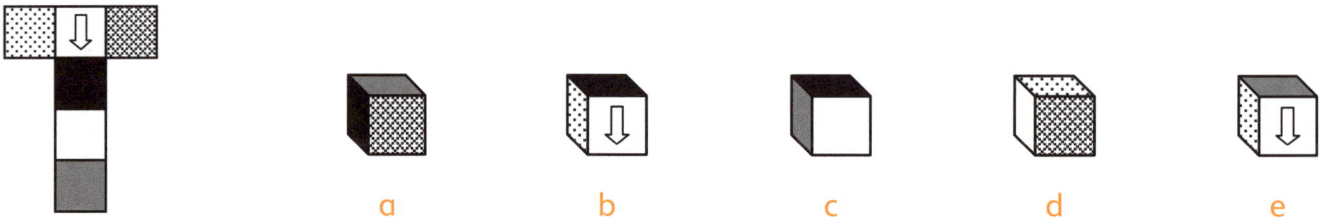

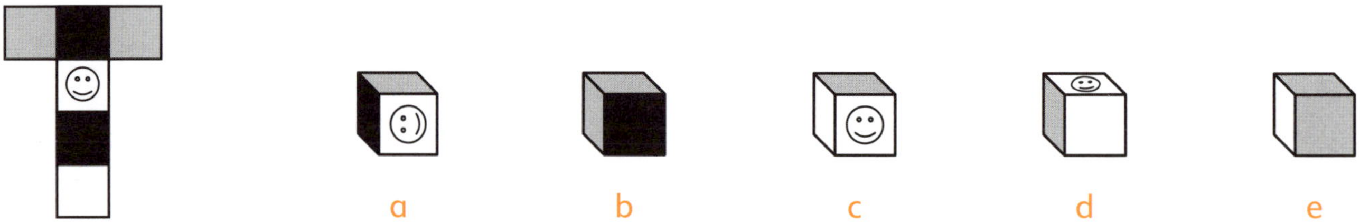

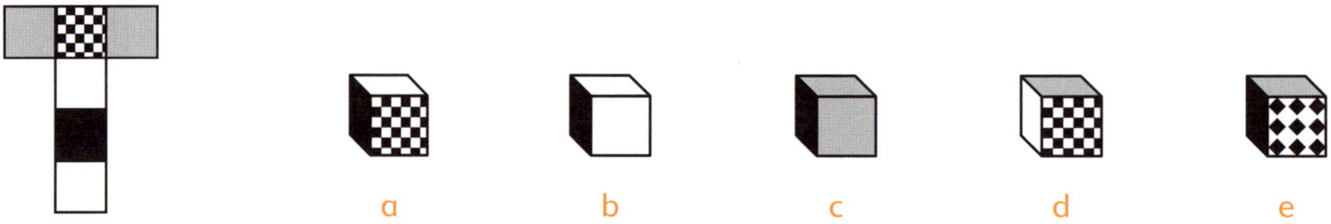

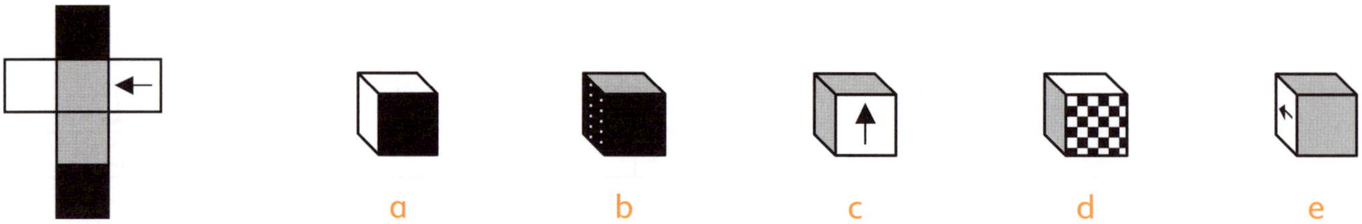

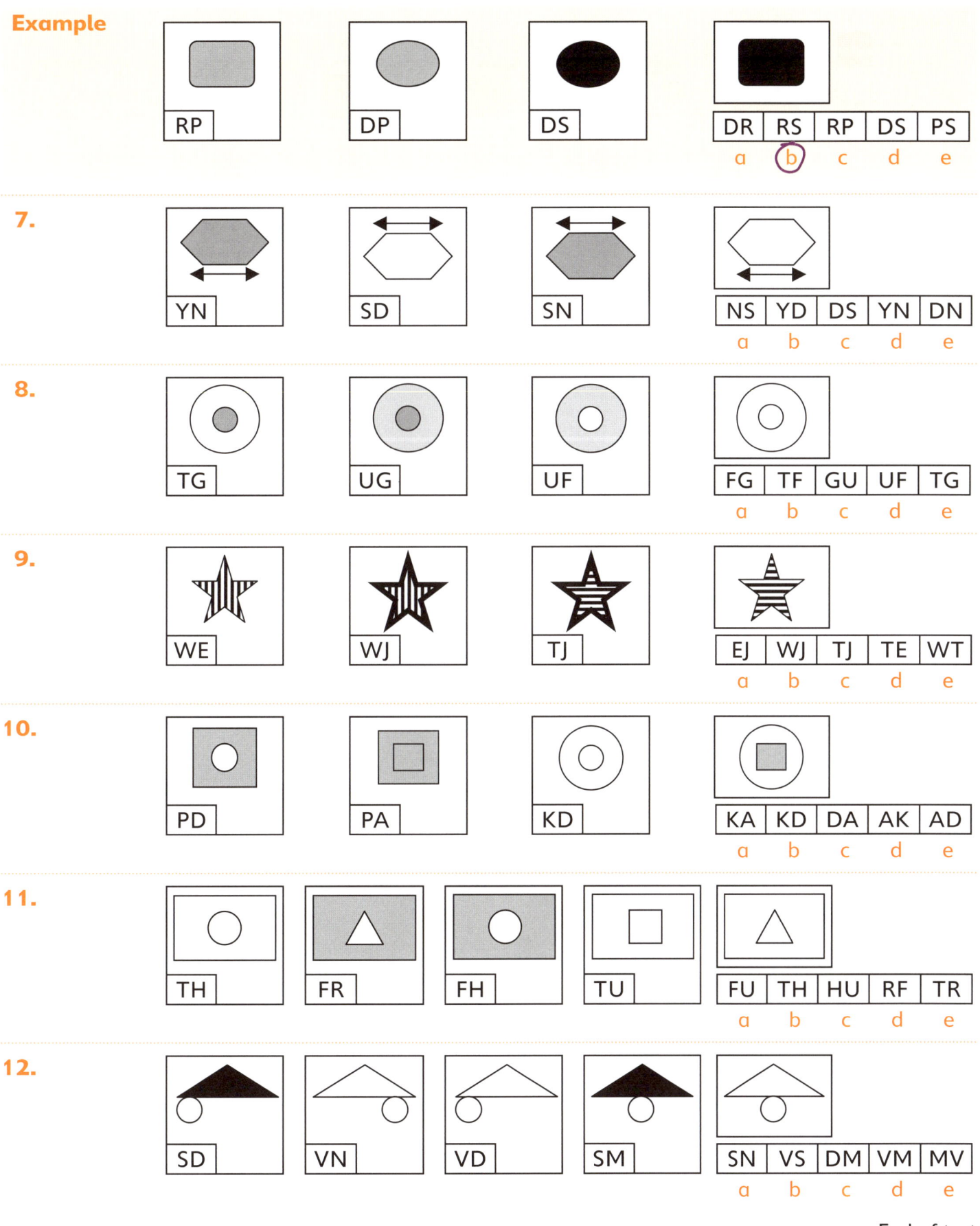

Section 2 Test 2

Target time: 6 minutes

Which picture on the right can be made by combining the two shapes on the left? Circle the letter.

Example

 + 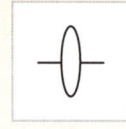 =
  a   b   **c**   d   e

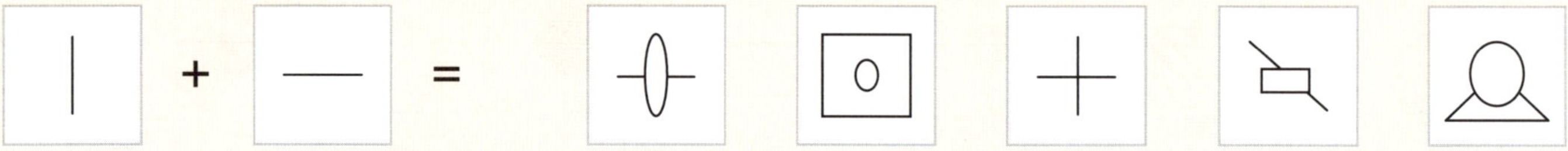

1. +  = 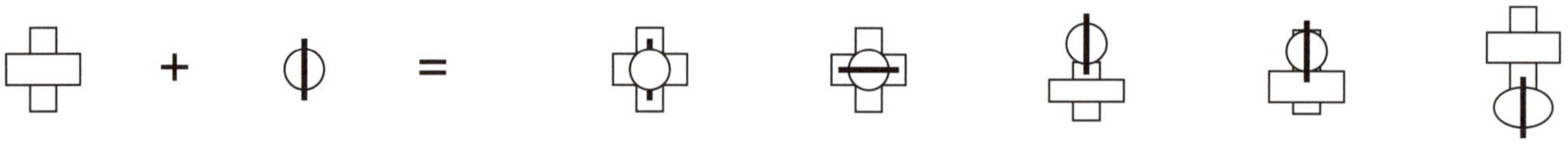
   a   b   c   d   e

2. 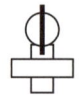 + 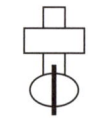 = 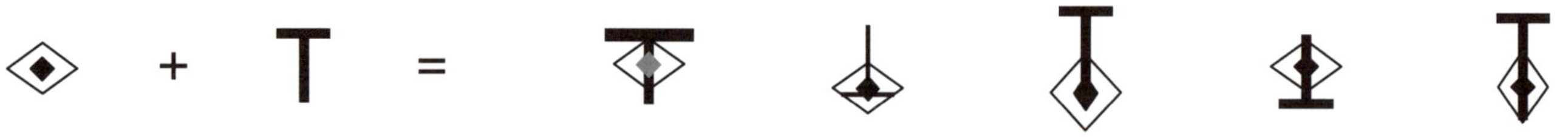
   a   b   c   d   e

3. + = 
   a   b   c   d   e

4.  +  = 
   a   b   c   d   e

5. +  = 
   a   b   c   d   e

6. + = 
   a   b   c   d   e

Now go on to the next page ➡

18   Schofield & Sims

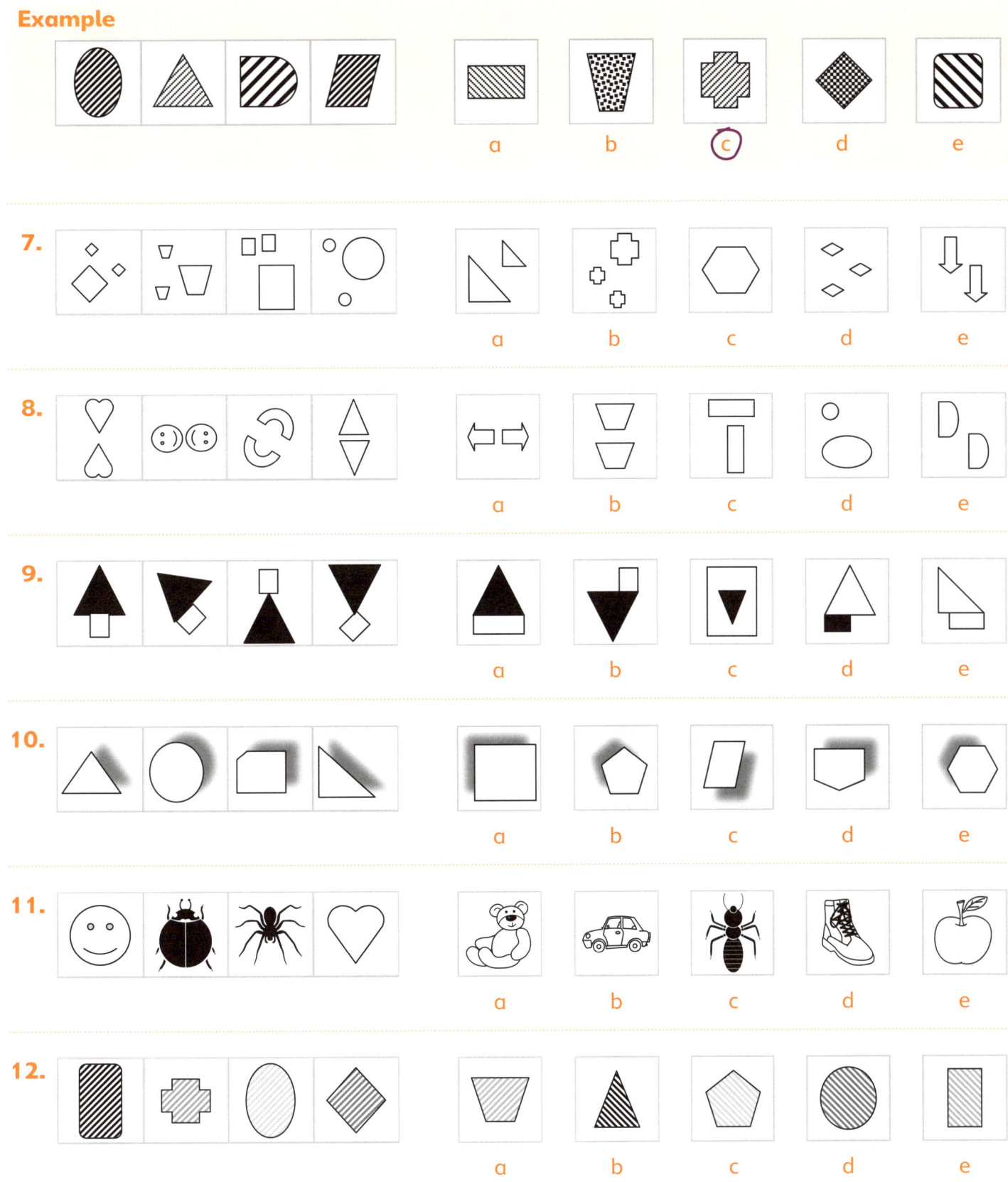

Section 2 Test 3

Target time: 6 minutes

Which picture is the odd one out? Circle the letter.

Example

 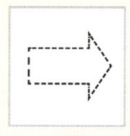  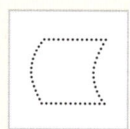 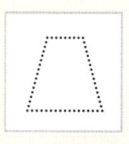

a   b   c   d   e

1.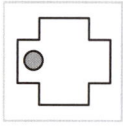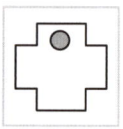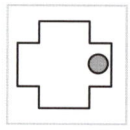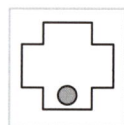

   a   b   c   d   e

2.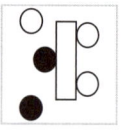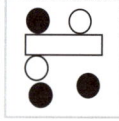

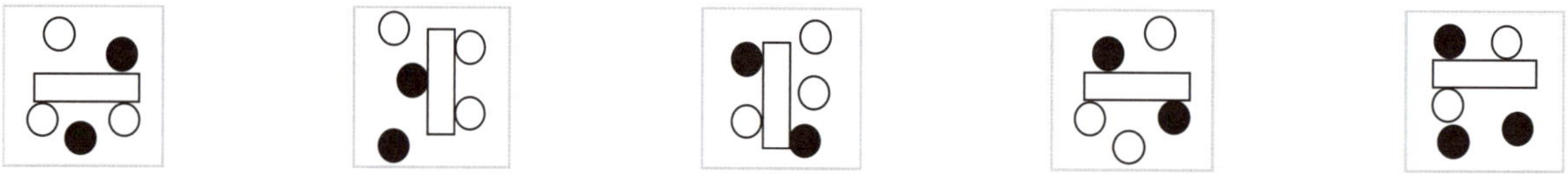

   a   b   c   d   e

3.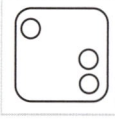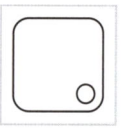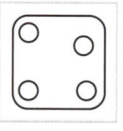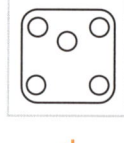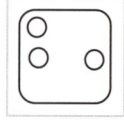

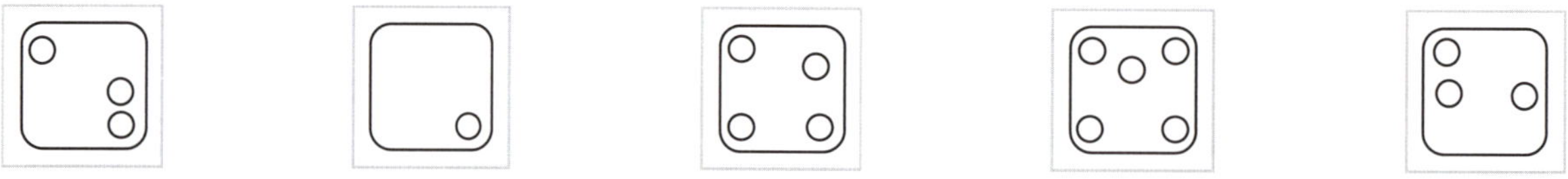

   a   b   c   d   e

4.

   a   b   c   d   e

5.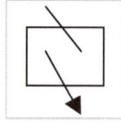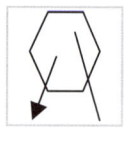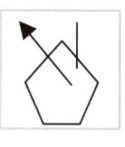

   a   b   c   d   e

6.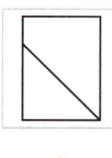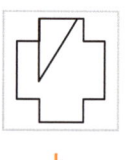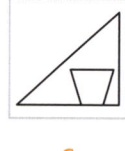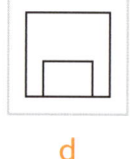

   a   b   c   d   e

Now go on to the next page ➡

Non-verbal Reasoning Rapid Tests 3 Answers

Notes for parents, tutors, teachers and other adult helpers

- **Non-verbal Reasoning Rapid Tests 3** is designed for eight- and nine-year-olds, but may also be suitable for some children of other ages.
- Remove this pull-out section before giving the book to the child.
- Before the child begins work on the first test, together read the instructions headed **What to do** on page 2. As you do so, point out to the child the different elements in **Section 1 Test 1**.
- Make sure that the child understands how to answer multiple choice questions and has a pencil, an eraser and a sheet of rough paper. Also ensure that the child is able to see a clock or a watch.
- Explain to the child how they should go about timing the test. Alternatively, you may wish to time the test yourself. When the child has finished the test, together work out the **Time taken** and complete the box that appears at the end of the test.
- Mark the child's work using this pull-out section, giving one mark for each correct answer. There are a total of 12 marks available for each test. Then complete the **Score** box at the end of the test.
- This table shows you how to mark the **Target met?** box and the **Action** notes help you to plan the next step. However, these are suggestions only. Please use your own judgement as you decide how best to proceed.

Score	Time taken	Target met?	Action
1–6	Any	Not yet	Give the child the previous book in the series. Provide help and support as needed.
7–9	Any	Not yet	Encourage the child to keep practising using the tests in this book. The child may need to repeat some tests. If so, wait a few weeks or the child may simply remember the correct answers. Provide help and support as needed.
10–12	Over target – child took too long	Not yet	
10–12	On target – child took suggested time or less	Yes	Encourage the child to keep practising using further tests in this book, and to move on to the next book when you think this is appropriate.

- After finishing each test, the child should fill in the **Progress chart** on page 40.
- Whatever the test score, always encourage the child to have another go at the questions that they got wrong – without looking at the solutions. If the child's answers are still incorrect, work through these questions together. Demonstrate the correct method if necessary.
- If the child struggles with particular question types, help them to develop the strategies needed.

Answers

Section 1 Test 1
(pages 4–5)

1. **d** Each picture contains a circle and arrow of the same colour.
2. **e** Each shows a right-angled triangle.
3. **a** Each picture contains a grey striped shape.
4. **b** Each picture contains a light grey 3D shape.
5. **c** Each large shape has a diamond inside it.
6. **c** Each picture contains a black shape with three lines sticking out.
7. **e** The others are all symmetrical.
8. **a** The others all have a curved side.
9. **b** The others all have a thick black outline and two white shapes inside.
10. **b** The others all have a total of 11 sides.
11. **d** The others all have lines that are shorter than the big rectangle.
12. **d** The arc on all the others is the same way up.

Section 1 Test 2
(pages 6–7)

1. **d** Both the shape and lines are reflected.
2. **a** The black picture becomes smaller and grey.
3. **a** The shape is reflected in the vertical mirror line, the outer line changes from solid to dashed, and the colour changes from white to grey.
4. **e** The picture is rotated 90° anticlockwise.
5. **c** There are the same number of lines as legs on the creature.
6. **c** The picture is reflected in the horizontal mirror line.
7. **b** The picture is rotated 45° clockwise.
8. **d** There is one less small circle each time and their colour alternates.
9. **e** Repeating pattern
10. **b** Repeating pattern
11. **d** The picture is rotated 90° anticlockwise and gets smaller each time.
12. **e** There are two more small triangles each time.

Section 1 Test 3
(pages 8–9)

1. **e**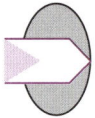
2. **c**
3. **d**
4. **b**
5. **a**
6. **d**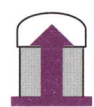
7. **d**
8. **b**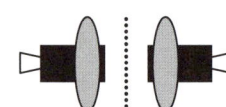
9. **c**
10. **b**
11. **c**
12. **d**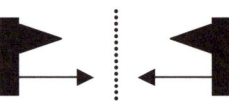

Answers

Section 1 Test 4 (pages 10–11)

1. e The shape gets smaller.
2. b The shape gets smaller and paler.
3. c The picture is reflected in the horizontal mirror line and gets smaller.
4. d The picture is reflected.
5. a The picture is reflected.
6. e The picture is reflected.
7. b
8. a
9. b
10. c
11. c
12. d

Section 1 Test 5 (pages 12–13)

If in doubt about the nets of cubes, copy them onto a piece of paper and fold them up.

1. a
2. e
3. e
4. d
5. d
6. c
7. e
8. e
9. a
10. d
11. b
12. b

Section 1 Test 6 (pages 14–15)

1. a First letter – shape
      Second letter – colour
2. b First letter – direction of arrow
      Second letter – colour
3. c First letter – colour
      Second letter – shape
4. d First letter – shape
      Second letter – colour
5. d First letter – colour
      Second letter – shape
6. c First letter – direction of arrow
      Second letter – colour
7. a First letter – shape
      Second letter – colour
8. e First letter – colour
      Second letter – outline
9. a First letter – shape
      Second letter – direction of stripes
10. e First letter – colour of rectangle
       Second letter – position of circle
11. b First letter – colour of oval
       Second letter – colour of rectangle
12. c First letter – direction of triangle
       Second letter – direction of arrow

Section 2 Test 1 (pages 16–17)

If in doubt about the nets of cubes, copy them onto a piece of paper and fold them up.

1. a
2. b
3. e
4. a
5. d
6. c
7. b First letter – position of arrow
      Second letter – colour
8. b First letter – colour of outer circle
      Second letter – colour of inner circle
9. d First letter – direction of stripes
      Second letter – outline
10. a First letter – outer shape
       Second letter – inner shape
11. e First letter – colour
       Second letter – inner shape
12. d First letter – colour
       Second letter – position of circle

Non-verbal Reasoning Rapid Tests 3 Answers

A3

Answers

Section 2 Test 2
(pages 18–19)

1. b
2. d
3. e
4. a
5. c
6. e
7. b Each picture contains a large shape and two smaller identical shapes.
8. a Each picture contains a pair of reflected shapes.
9. b Each picture contains the same black triangle and white rectangle.
10. d Each picture contains a shape with a shadow to the top right.
11. c Each picture has a line of symmetry.
12. a Each picture contains stripes going in the same direction.

Section 2 Test 3
(pages 20–21)

1. c The other crosses are all upright.
2. e The others all have two black circles and three white circles.
3. c The others all have an odd number of circles.
4. b The others are all quadrilaterals.
5. c The others all have an arrow pointing outwards from the shape.
6. d The other pictures all contain a triangle somewhere.
7. a The picture is rotated 90° anticlockwise.
8. e The picture is reflected in the horizontal mirror line.
9. d The picture is rotated 90° anticlockwise.
10. b A third of the picture remains and changes from white to black.
11. b The picture is reflected in the horizontal mirror line and the shapes swap colours.
12. a The picture is reflected in the vertical mirror line and changes from white to black.

Section 2 Test 4
(pages 22–23)

1. a The picture gets smaller and the direction of the arrow alternates.
2. c The picture gets smaller and its direction alternates.
3. b There is one extra grey oval each time.
4. b The circle moves round clockwise and gets lighter each time.
5. c Repeating pattern
6. c An oval is added each time and the colour of the ovals alternates.
7. d
8. e
9. c
10. b
11. a
12. e

Answers

Section 2 Test 5
(pages 24–25)
1. **e** The picture is reflected.
2. **c** The picture is reflected.
3. **b** The arrow is rotated 90° clockwise.
4. **e** The picture is rotated 90° anticlockwise.
5. **b** The picture is rotated 180°.
6. **c** The picture is reflected.
7. **c**
8. **d**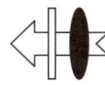
9. **b**
10. **a**
11. **d**
12. **d**

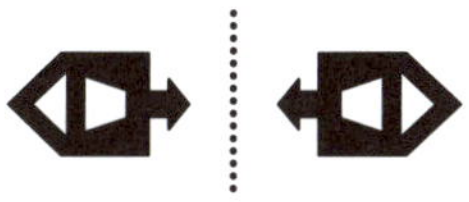

Section 2 Test 6
(pages 26–27)
If in doubt about the nets of cubes, copy them onto a piece of paper and fold them up.
1. **d**
2. **e**
3. **b**
4. **b**
5. **a**
6. **e**
7. **a** First letter – outer shape
   Second letter – colour of oval
8. **c** First letter – star shape
   Second letter – number of circles
9. **c** First letter – outer shape
   Second letter – position of line
10. **a** First letter – colour of cross
    Second letter – position of line
11. **d** First letter – direction of arrow
    Second letter – shape
12. **e** First letter – colour of triangle
    Second letter – colour of star

Section 3 Test 1
(pages 28–29)
1. **c** Each picture contains two triangles on one side of the line and one triangle on the other side of the line.
2. **d** Each picture contains a thin black arrow and a wide white arrow on opposite sides of the line.
3. **e** Each picture contains at least one set of parallel lines. (Or they have an even number of sides.)
4. **b** Each picture contains a white cross, a black oval and a black triangle.
5. **a** Each picture contains eight white ovals and two black ovals.
6. **b** Each picture contains four arrow heads.
7. **b** The others all have eight sides.
8. **a** The others are all single-headed arrows.
9. **d** The others have a line of symmetry.
10. **c** The others are all rotations of the same shape, but **c** is a reflection.
11. **e** The others are all hexagons (six-sided shapes).
12. **d** The others all have the same type of dashed line.

Non-verbal Reasoning Rapid Tests 3 Answers

A5

Answers

Section 3 Test 2
(pages 30–31)

1. **a** The picture is rotated 90° clockwise.
2. **d** The picture is rotated 90° clockwise (and the stripes rotate with it).
3. **e** The picture is rotated 90° clockwise, gets smaller and changes from black to grey.
4. **b** The smaller shape becomes larger and the larger shape becomes smaller.
5. **c** The shape is rotated 90° clockwise.
6. **b** The picture and stripes are reflected in the horizontal mirror line.
7. **c** The picture is rotated 45° clockwise and gets lighter each time.
8. **a** An extra arrow is added each time, while the direction of the arrows alternates.
9. **e** The shape gets smaller and the type of shading alternates.
10. **c** The picture is rotated 45° clockwise.
11. **b** The stripes are rotated 45° clockwise.
12. **d** Repeating pattern

Section 3 Test 3
(pages 32–33)

1. **c**
2. **d**
3. **b**
4. **d**
5. **c**
6. **a**

7. **b**
8. **e**
9. **b**
10. **d**
11. **e**
12. **d** 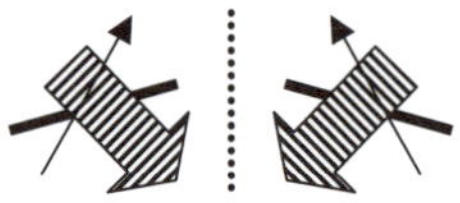 (note position of arrow and line)

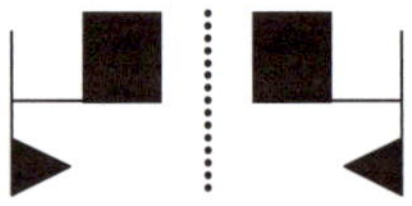

Section 3 Test 4
(pages 34–35)

1. **e** The picture is reflected.
2. **d** The picture is reflected.
3. **a** The same size shape is rotated 90° clockwise across the row so that shapes in the columns face the same way.
4. **b** The shape is rotated 90° clockwise and then back again, and it also changes from white to black and back to white.
5. **c** Reflective pattern
6. **a** Reflective pattern

Answers

7. d

8. c

9. b

10. d

11. c

12. e

Section 3 Test 5
(pages 36–37)

If in doubt about the nets of cubes, copy them onto a piece of paper and fold them up.

1. e
2. b
3. e
4. d
5. d
6. a
7. a First letter – direction of stripes
     Second letter – direction of arrow
8. d First letter – large shape
     Second letter – position of rectangle
9. a First letter – position of lines
     Second letter – colour
10. b First letter – position of circle
      Second letter – direction of arrow
11. c First letter – inside shape
      Second letter – outside shape
12. c First letter – number of lines
      Second letter – direction of arrow

Section 3 Test 6
(pages 38–39)

1. a

2. d

3. c

4. d

5. e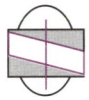

6. b

7. b The picture is rotated 90° clockwise.
8. a The picture is rotated slightly clockwise each time.
9. c The picture is rotated slightly anticlockwise each time.
10. e An extra diamond is added to each picture, starting from the top and moving clockwise.
11. d The circle moves clockwise around the rectangle and the spots on the rectangle become more dense.
12. d An extra triangle is added to each picture, starting from the top and moving clockwise. The direction of the triangles alternates each time.

Non-verbal Reasoning Rapid Tests 3 Answers

A7

This book of answers is a pull-out section from
Non-verbal Reasoning Rapid Tests 3
Published by **Schofield & Sims Ltd**,
7 Mariner Court, Wakefield, West Yorkshire WF4 3FL, UK
Telephone 01484 607080
www.schofieldandsims.co.uk

First published in 2014
This edition copyright © Schofield & Sims Ltd, 2018
Fifth impression 2021

Author: **Rebecca Brant**
Rebecca Brant has asserted her moral right under the Copyright, Designs and Patents Act, 1988, to be identified as the author of this work.

British Library Cataloguing in Publication Data
A catalogue record for this book is available from the British Library.

All rights reserved. No part of this publication may be reproduced, stored in a retrieval system, or transmitted in any form or by any means, electronic, mechanical, photocopying, recording or otherwise, without either the prior permission of the publisher or a licence permitting restricted copying in the United Kingdom issued by the Copyright Licensing Agency Ltd.

Commissioned by **Carolyn Richardson Publishing Services**

Design by **Oxford Designers & Illustrators**
Printed in the UK by **Page Bros (Norwich) Ltd**

ISBN 978 07217 1465 3

Section 2 Test 4

Target time: 6 minutes

Which picture on the right belongs to the group on the left? Circle the letter.

Example

     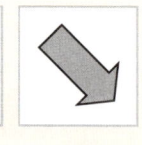

a   b   c   (d)   e

1.

a   b   c   d   e

2.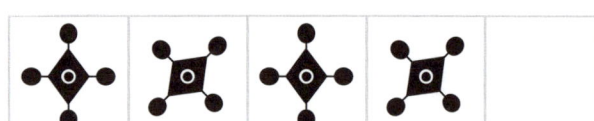

a   b   c   d   e

3.

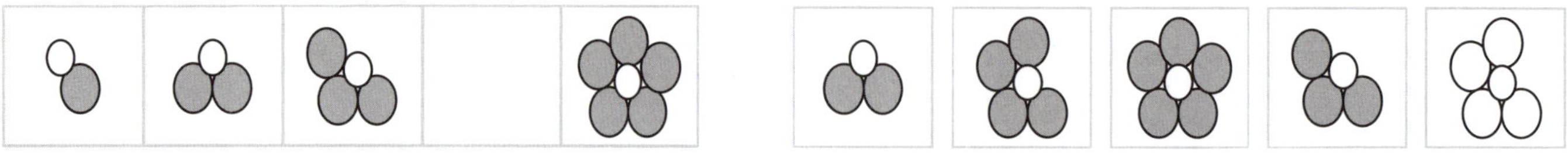

a   b   c   d   e

4.

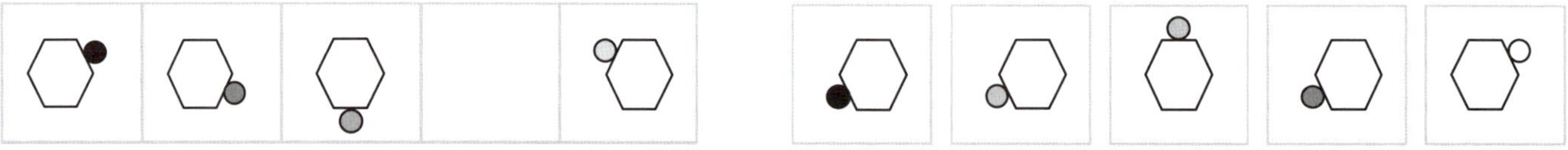

a   b   c   d   e

5.

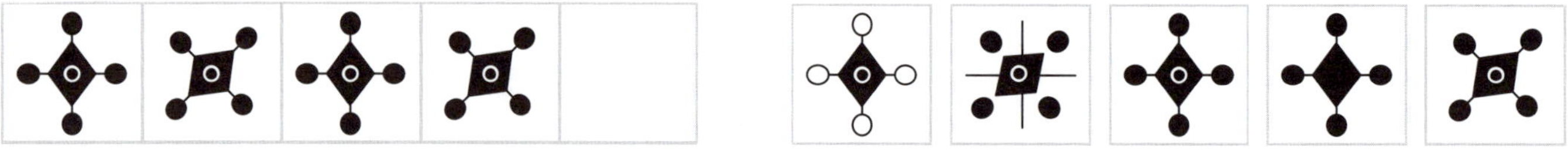

a   b   c   d   e

6.

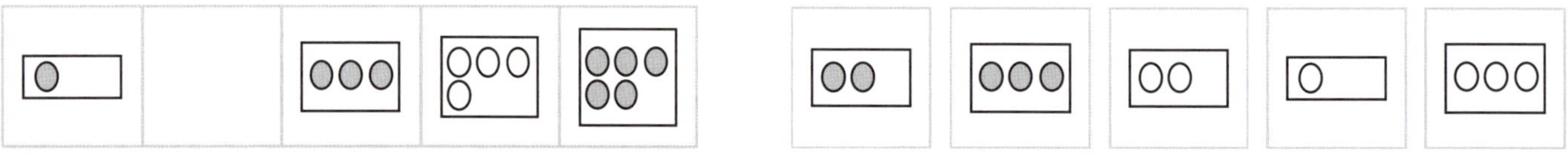

a   b   c   d   e

Now go on to the next page ➡

22

Section 2 Test 4 continued

In which picture on the right is the picture on the left hidden? Circle the letter.

Example

   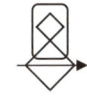      
　　　　　　a　　　　b　　　　c　　　　d　　　(e)

7.       　　　　　   　　　　
　　　　　　a　　　　b　　　　c　　　　d　　　　e

8.
　　　　　　a　　　　b　　　　c　　　　d　　　　e

9.
　　　　　　a　　　　b　　　　c　　　　d　　　　e

10.
　　　　　　a　　　　b　　　　c　　　　d　　　　e

11.      　　　　　
　　　　　　a　　　　b　　　　c　　　　d　　　　e

12.      　　　　　   　　　　
　　　　　　a　　　　b　　　　c　　　　d　　　　e

End of test

| Score: | Time taken: | Target met? |

Section 2 Test 5

Target time: 6 minutes

Which picture on the right best fits into the space in the grid on the left? Circle the letter.

Example

a b c (d) e

1.

a b c d e

2.

a b c d e

3.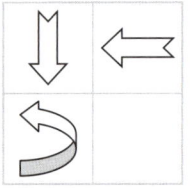

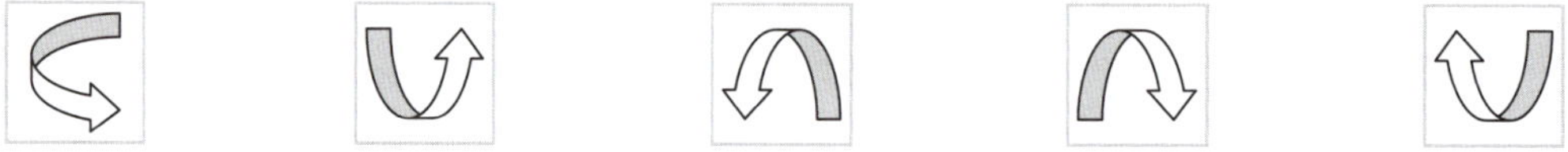

a b c d e

4.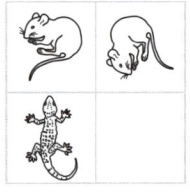

a b c d e

5.

a b c d e

6.

a b c d e

Now go on to the next page ➡

Section 2 Test 5 continued

Which picture on the right is a reflection of the picture on the left? Circle the letter.

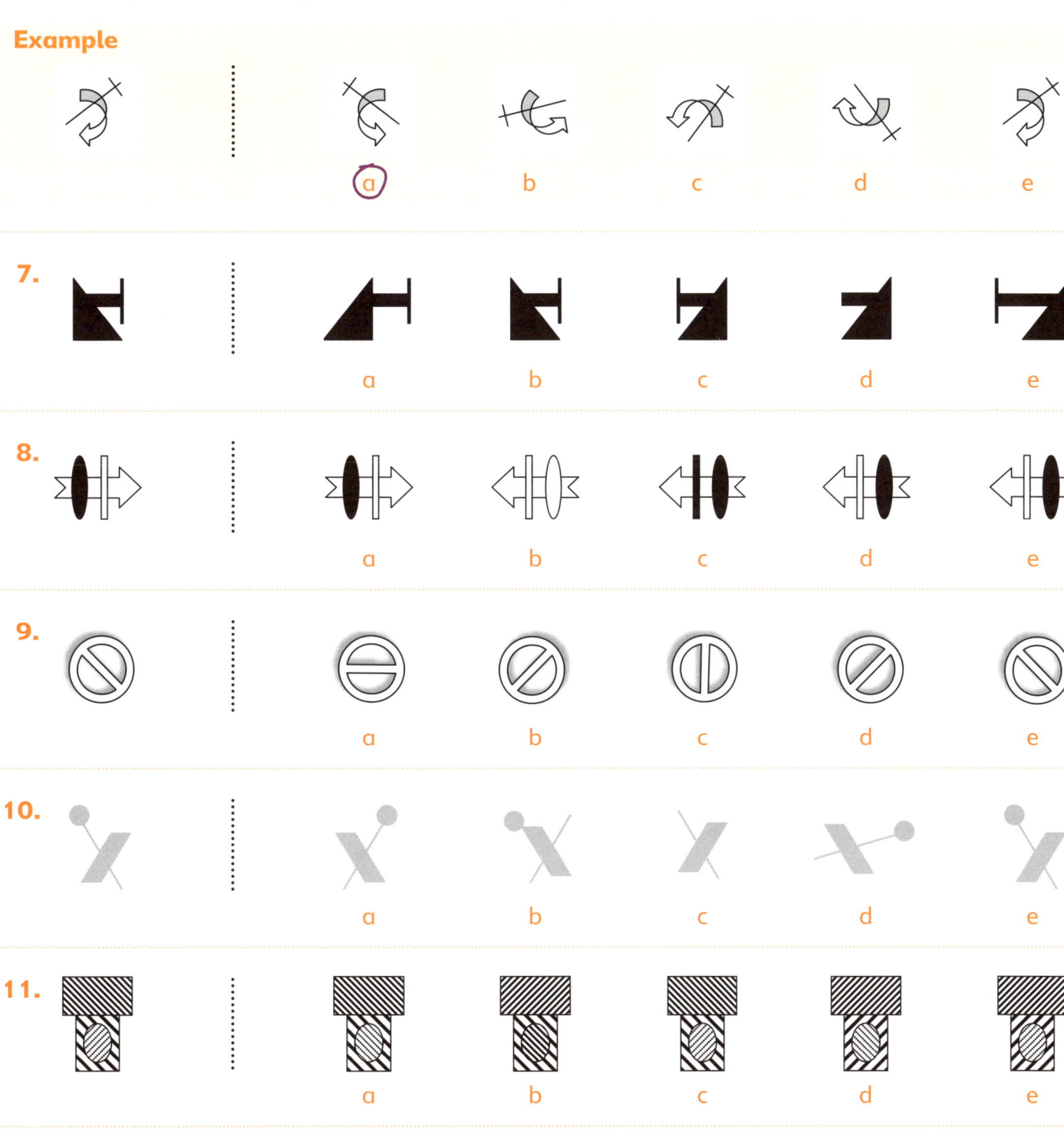

Section 2 Test 6

Target time: 6 minutes

Which net can be made from the cube? Circle the letter.

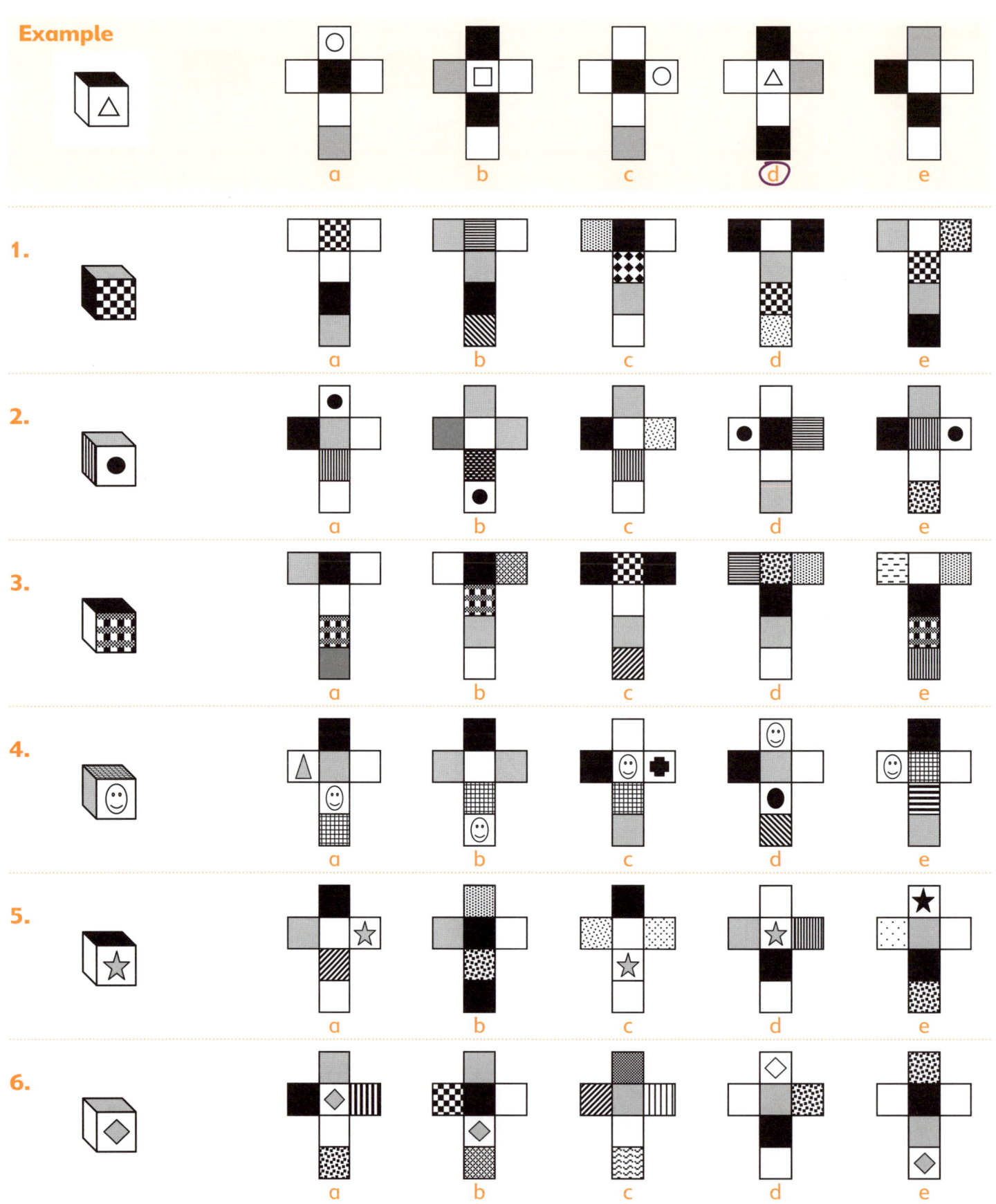

Now go on to the next page ➡

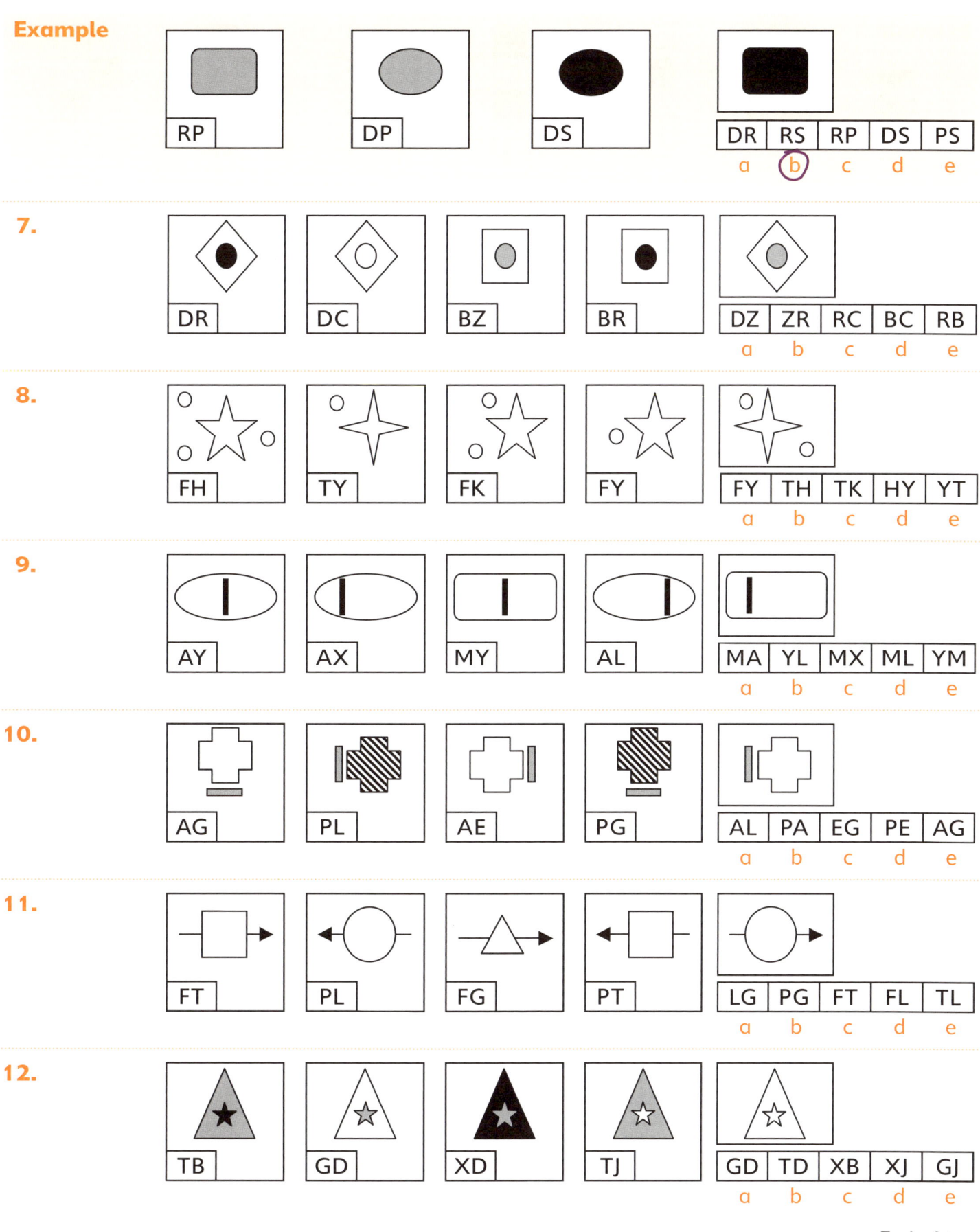

Section 3 Test 1

Target time: **6 minutes**

Which picture on the right belongs to the group on the left? Circle the letter.

Example

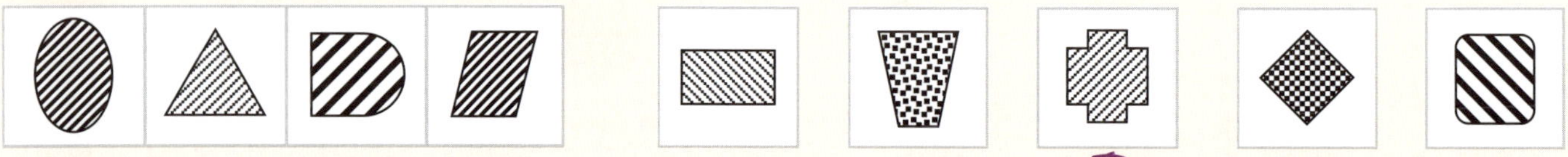

a   b   c   d   e

1.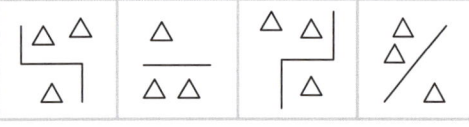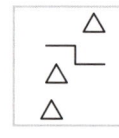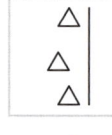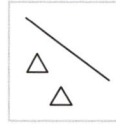

a   b   c   d   e

2.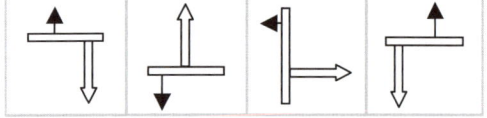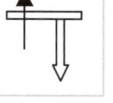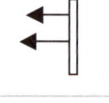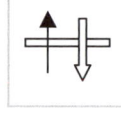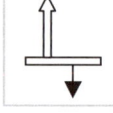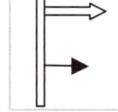

a   b   c   d   e

3.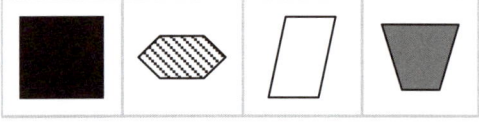

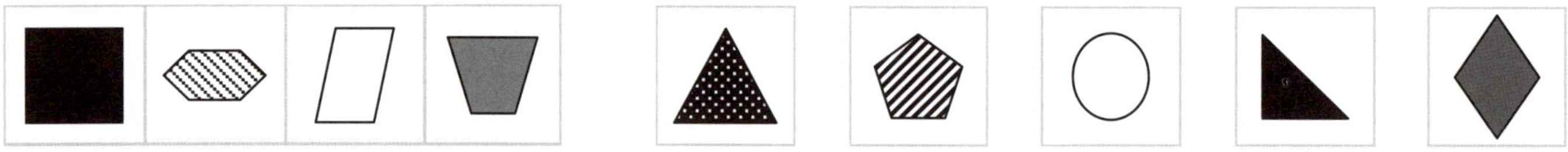

a   b   c   d   e

4.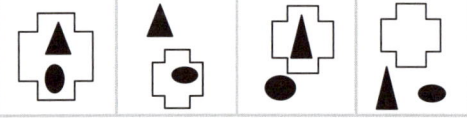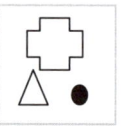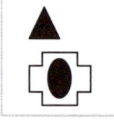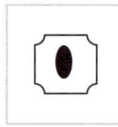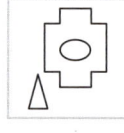

a   b   c   d   e

5.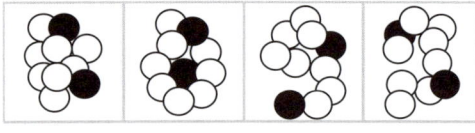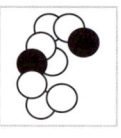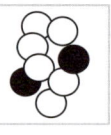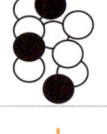

a   b   c   d   e

6.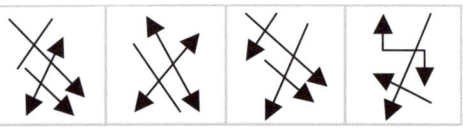

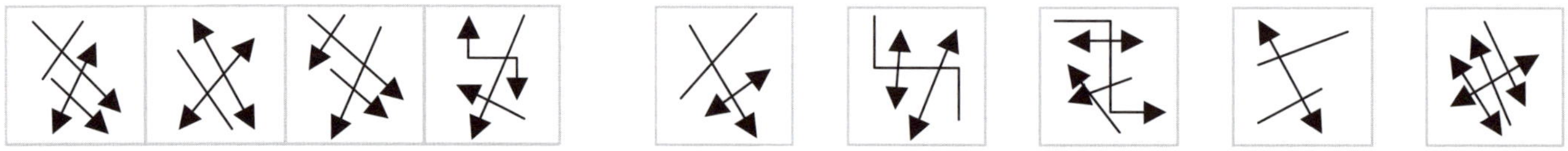

a   b   c   d   e

Now go on to the next page ➡

Section **3** Test **1**
continued

Which picture is the odd one out? Circle the letter.

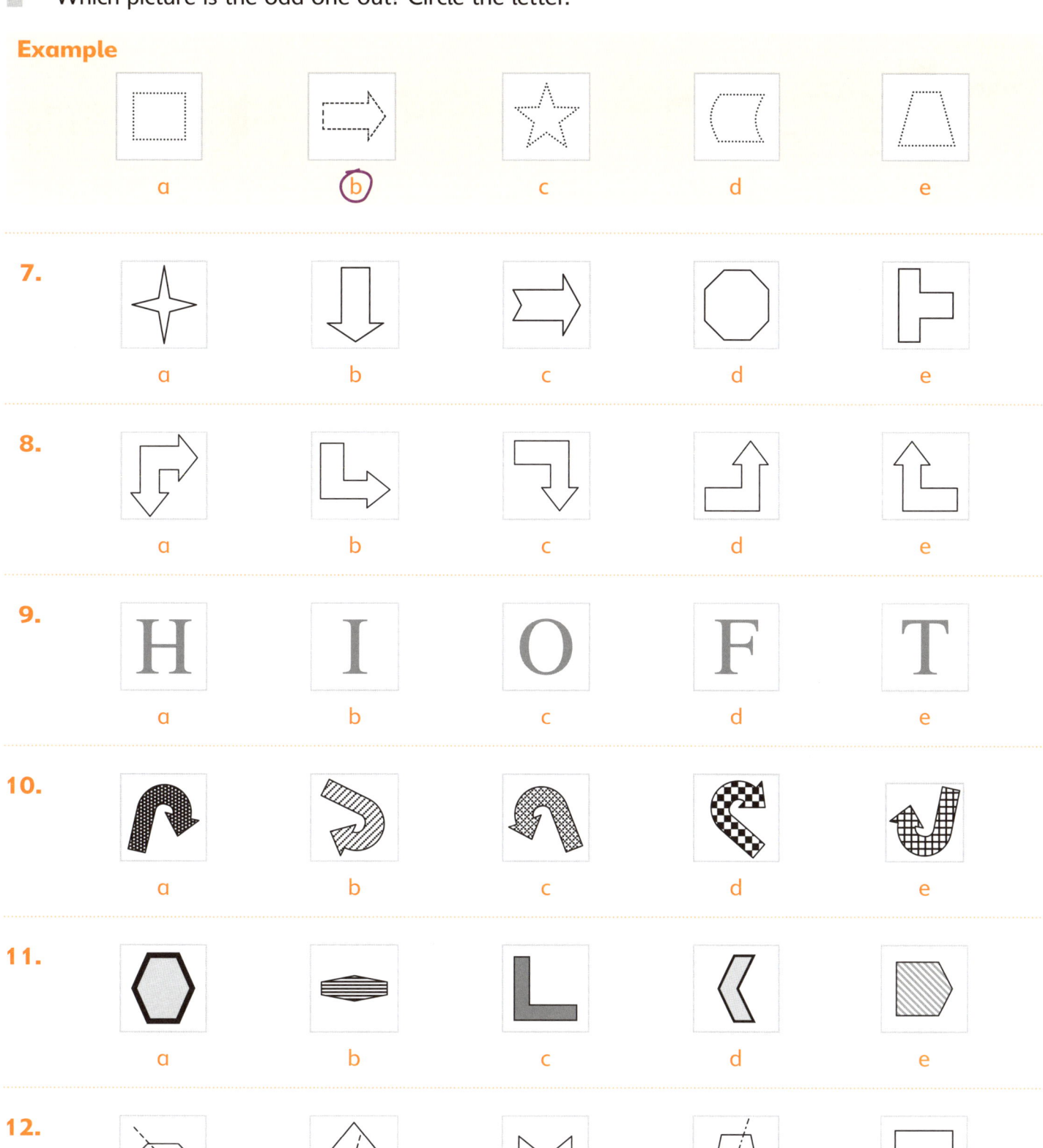

Example

7.

8.

9.

10.

11.

12.

End of test

Score: Time taken: Target met?

Non-verbal Reasoning Rapid Tests 3   29

Section 3 Test 2

Target time: 6 minutes

There is a pair of pictures on the left. Which one of the five pictures on the right goes with the single picture on the left to make a pair in the same way? Circle the letter.

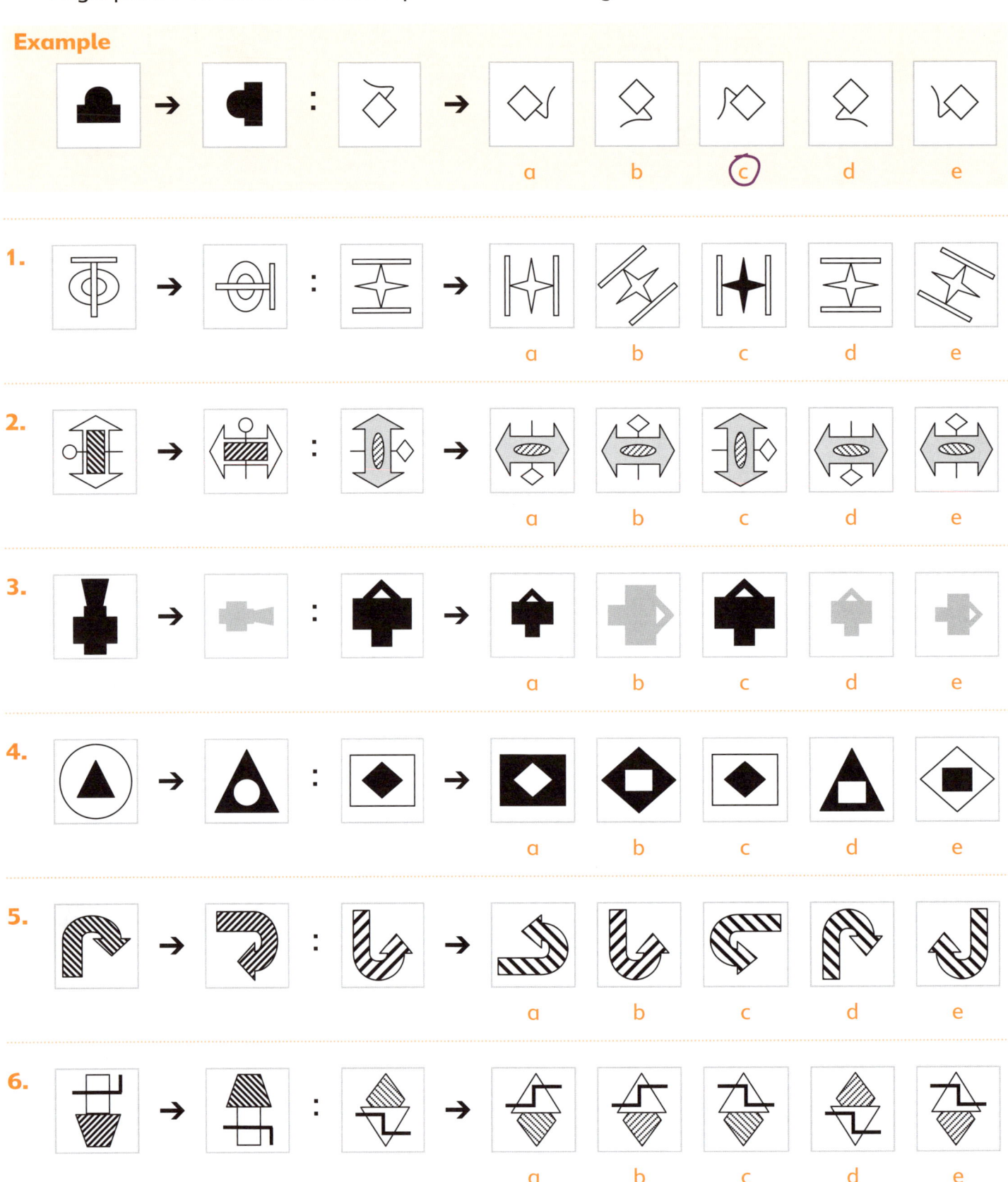

Example

Section 3 Test 2 continued

Which picture on the right belongs to the group on the left? Circle the letter.

Example

7.

8.

9.

10.

11.

12.

End of test

Score: Time taken: Target met?

Non-verbal Reasoning Rapid Tests 3   31

Section 3 Test 3

Target time: 6 minutes

In which picture on the right is the picture on the left hidden? Circle the letter.

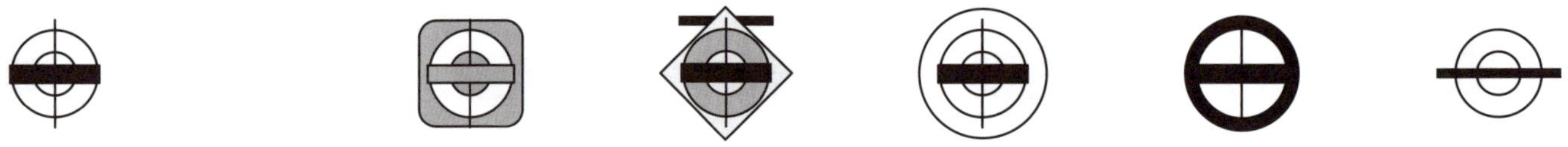

Section 3 Test 3
continued

Which picture on the right is a reflection of the picture on the left? Circle the letter.

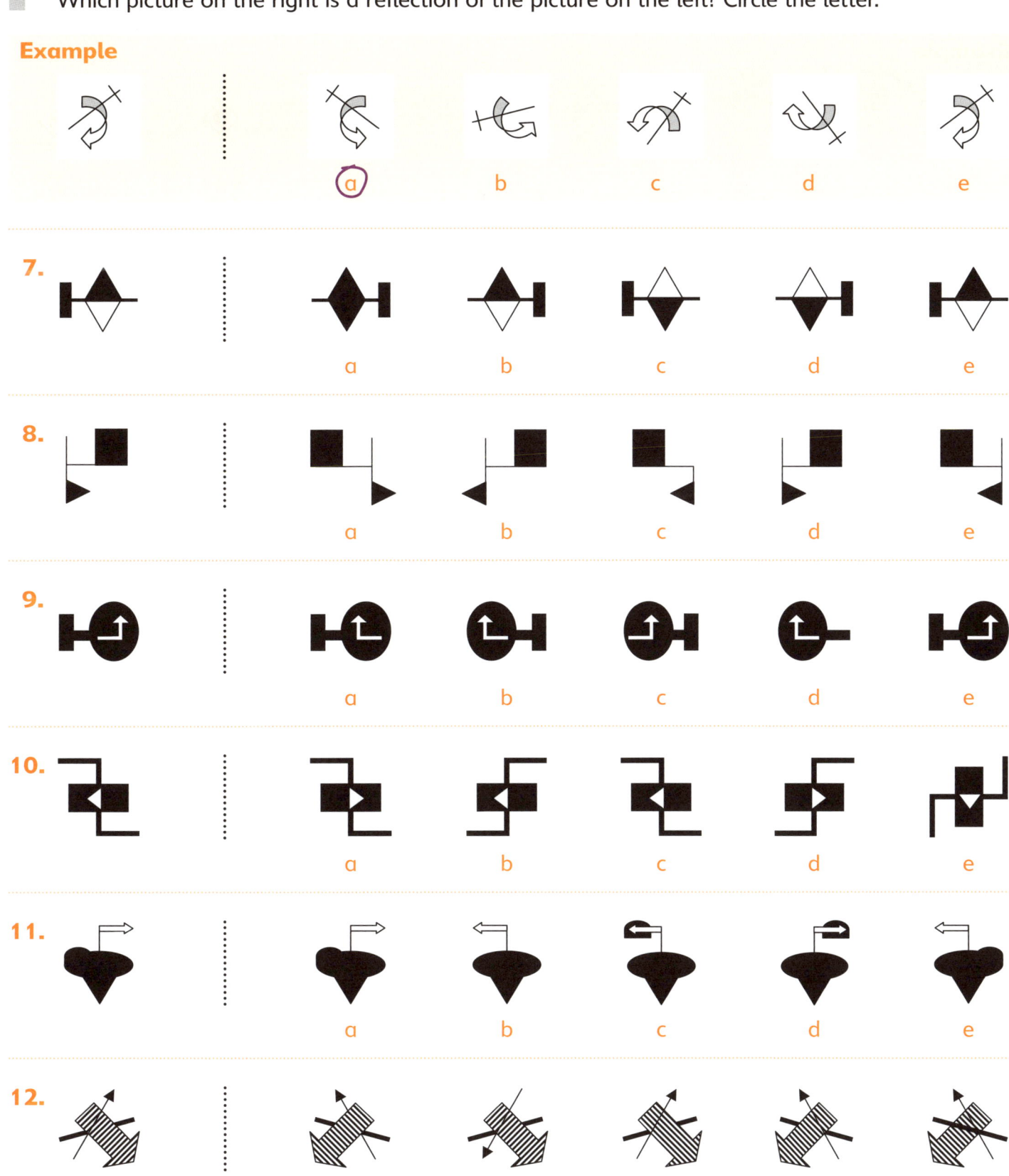

Example

7.

8.

9.

10.

11.

12.

End of test

Score: Time taken: Target met?

Non-verbal Reasoning Rapid Tests 3   33

Section 3 Test 4

Target time: 6 minutes

Which picture on the right best fits into the space in the grid on the left? Circle the letter.

Example

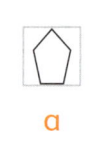

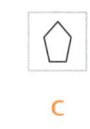

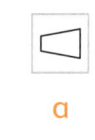

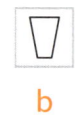

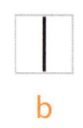

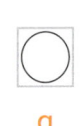

1. 
2. 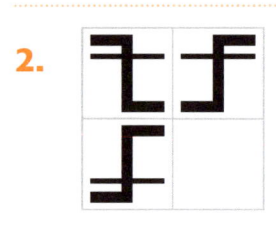
3. 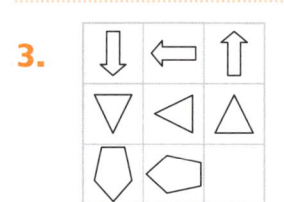
4. 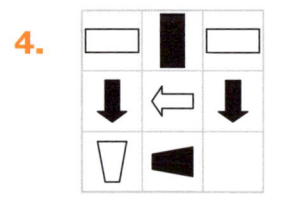
5. 
6.

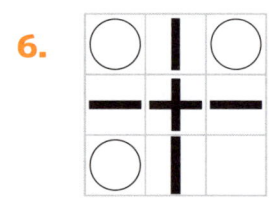

Now go on to the next page

Section 3 Test 4 continued

Which picture on the right can be made by combining the two shapes on the left? Circle the letter.

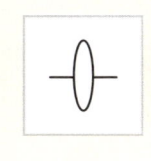

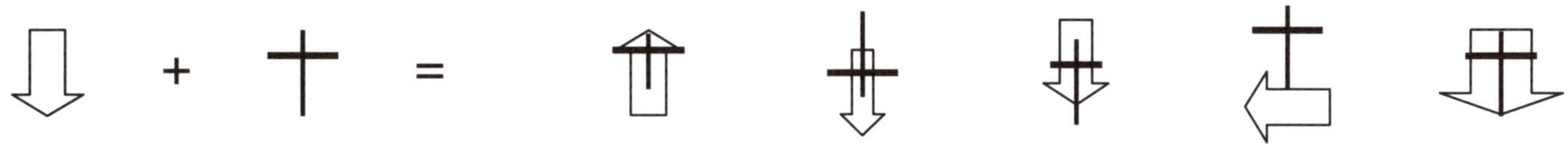

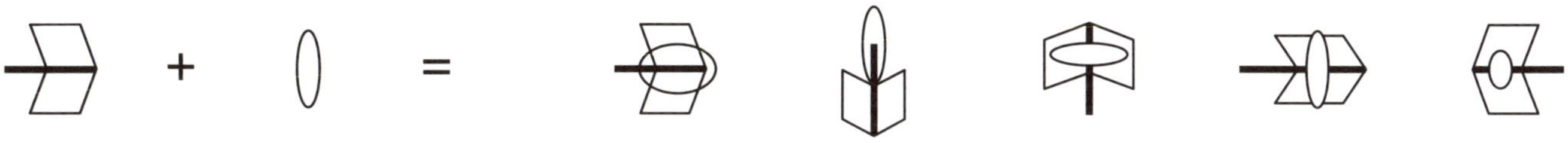

Example

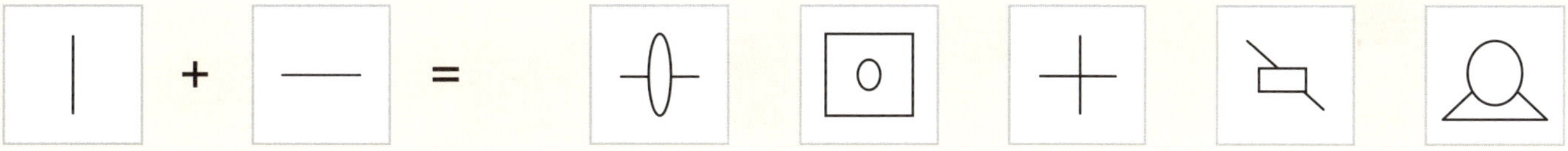

7.

8.

9.

10.

11.

12.

End of test

Score: Time taken: Target met?

Section 3 Test 5

Target time: 6 minutes

Which net can be made from the cube? Circle the letter.

Example

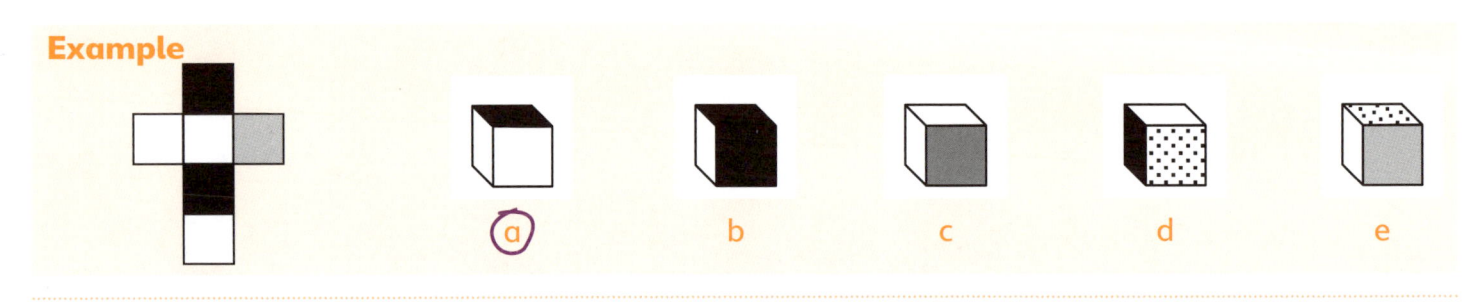

a (circled)   b   c   d   e

1. a   b   c   d   e

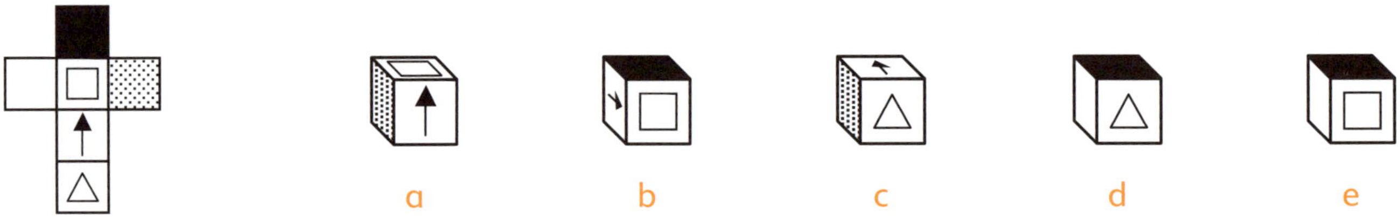

2. a   b   c   d   e

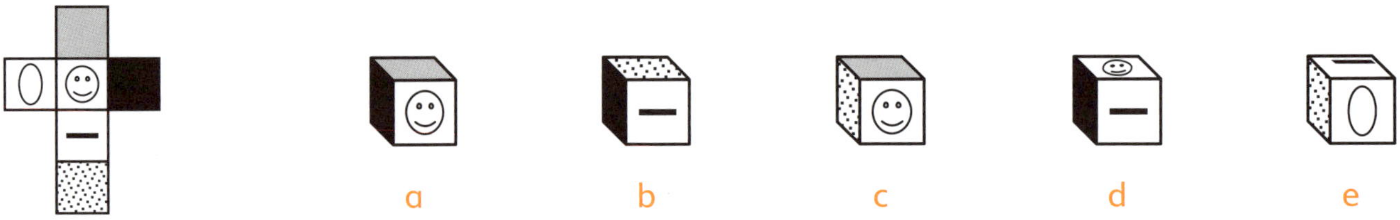

3. a   b   c   d   e

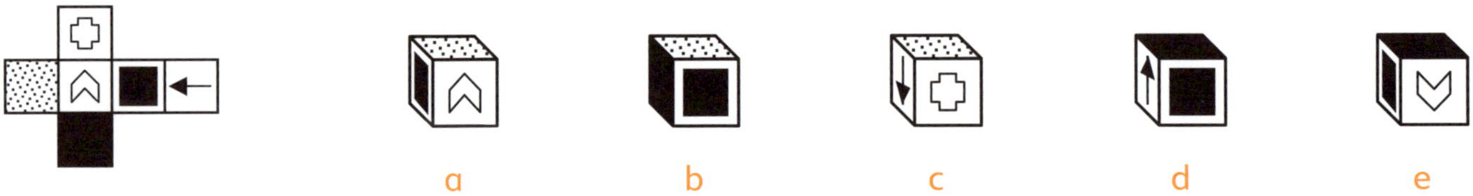

4. a   b   c   d   e

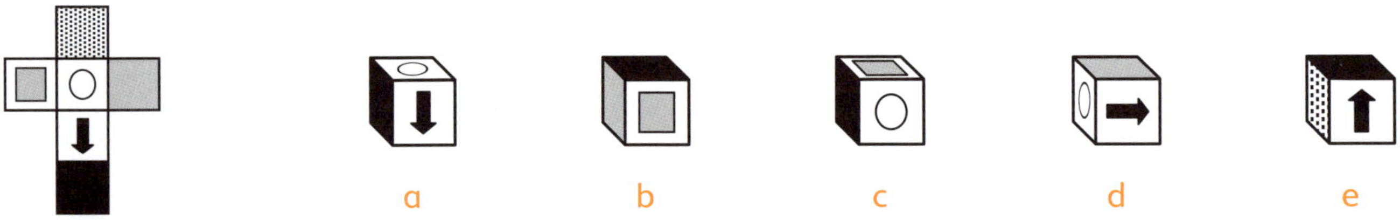

5. a   b   c   d   e

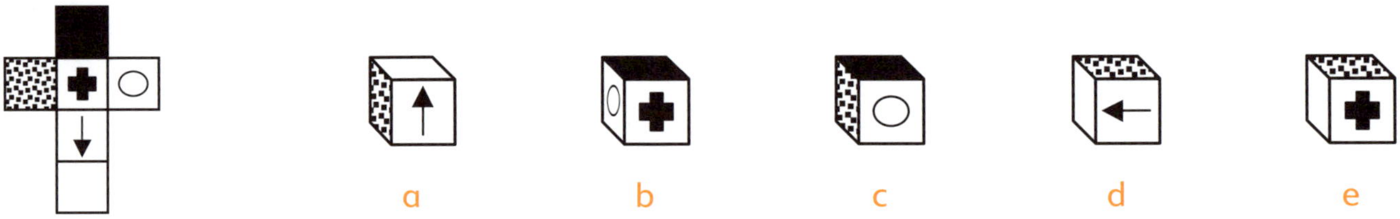

6. a   b   c   d   e

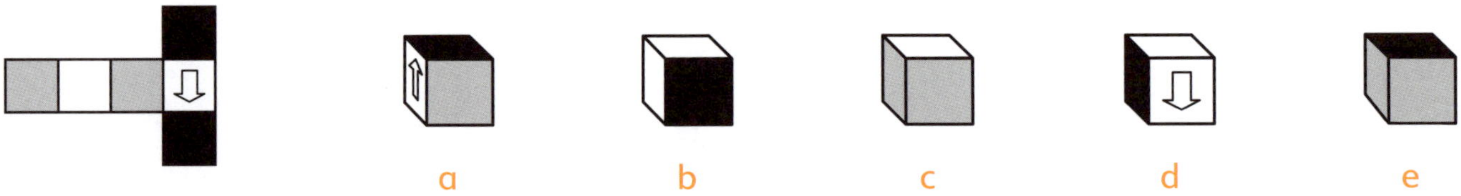

Now go on to the next page ➡

Section 3 Test 5 continued

What is the code of the final picture? Circle the letter.

Example

RP	DP	DS	DR	RS	RP	DS	PS
			a	(b)	c	d	e

7.

SN	KR	SR	GN	KN	GR	GN	KS	SK
				a	b	c	d	e

8.

DH	RU	DW	BH	BW	DU	RH	RW	BU
				a	b	c	d	e

9.

VC	MJ	TJ	MX	TC	MJ	VJ	TX	VX
				a	b	c	d	e

10.

QH	LH	QA	CF	CA	LA	QF	LF	CH
				a	b	c	d	e

11.

NX	ML	ND	PL	MD	NL	PX	MX	PD
				a	b	c	d	e

12.

TH	TG	DH	CM	DM	CH	TM	CG	DG
				a	b	c	d	e

End of test

Score: Time taken: Target met?

Non-verbal Reasoning Rapid Tests 3

Section 3 Test 6

Target time: 6 minutes

In which picture on the right is the picture on the left hidden? Circle the letter.

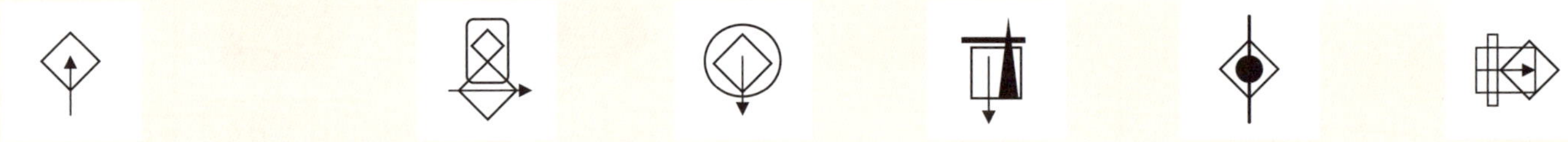

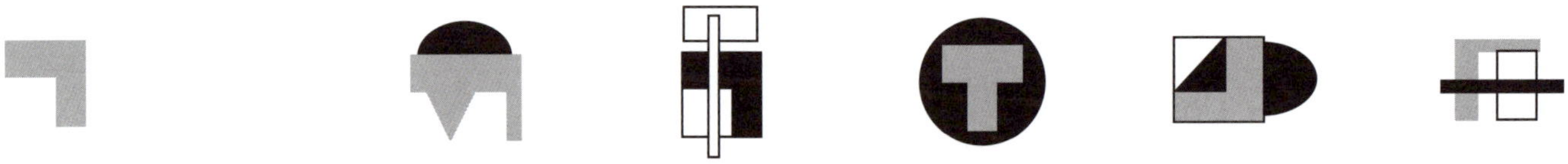

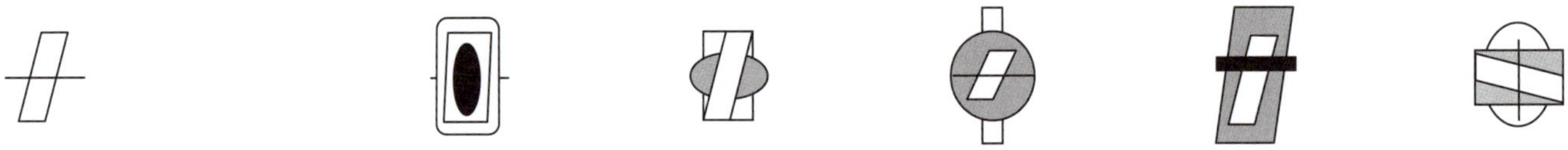

Section **3** Test **6**
continued

Which picture on the right belongs to the group on the left? Circle the letter.

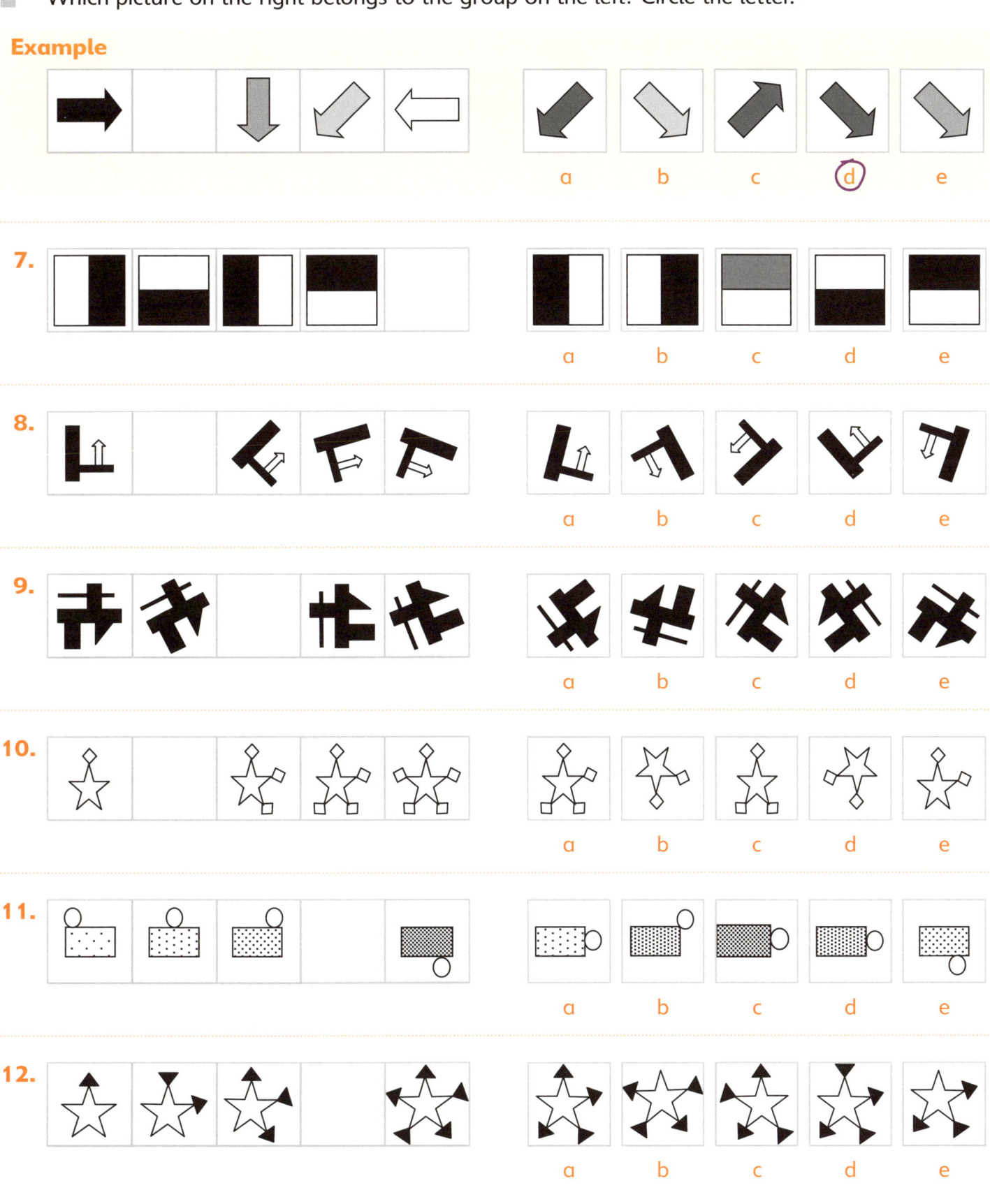

Example

7.

8.

9.

10.

11.

12.

End of test

Score: Time taken: Target met?

Non-verbal Reasoning Rapid Tests 3   39

Progress chart

Write the score (out of 12) for each test in the box provided on the right of the graph.
Then colour in the row next to the box to represent this score.

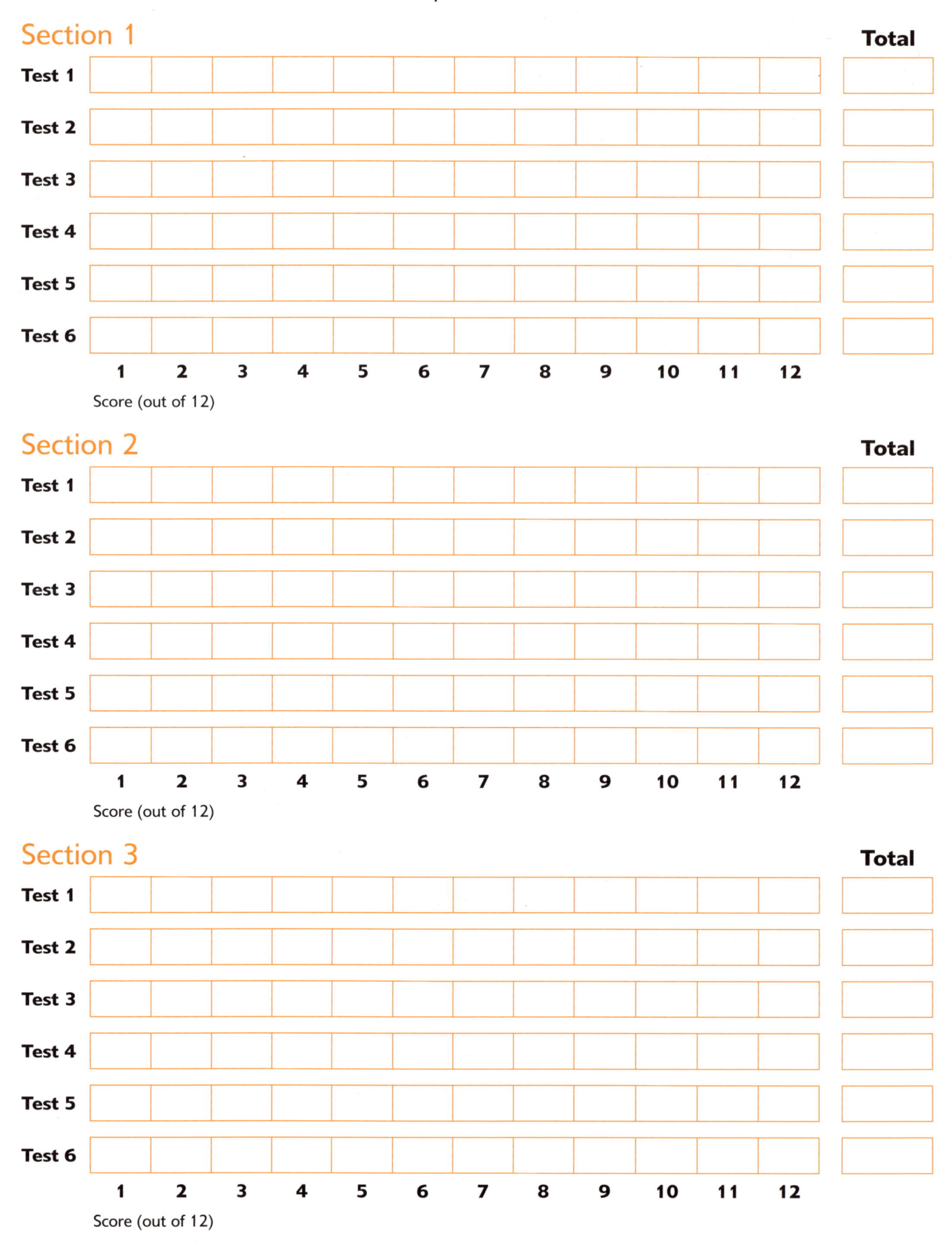

Section 1
Total

Test 1
Test 2
Test 3
Test 4
Test 5
Test 6

1 2 3 4 5 6 7 8 9 10 11 12
Score (out of 12)

Section 2
Total

Test 1
Test 2
Test 3
Test 4
Test 5
Test 6

1 2 3 4 5 6 7 8 9 10 11 12
Score (out of 12)

Section 3
Total

Test 1
Test 2
Test 3
Test 4
Test 5
Test 6

1 2 3 4 5 6 7 8 9 10 11 12
Score (out of 12)